Mammoth Cave by Lantern Light

Visiting America's Most Famous Cave in the 1800s

Mammoth Cave by Lantern Light

Visiting America's Most Famous Cave in the 1800s

Colleen O'Connor Olson

Cave Books, Dayton, Ohio

Library of Congress Control Number 2010012533
ISBN 978-0-939748-75-4

First Edition August 2010

Library of Congress Cataloging-in-Publication Data

Olson, Colleen O'Connor, 1966-

Mammoth Cave by lantern light : visiting America's most famous
    cave in the 1800s / Colleen O'Connor Olson.
    p. cm.
Includes bibliographical references and index.

ISBN-13: 978-0-939748-75-4 (pbk. : alk. paper)
ISBN-10: 0-939748-75-4 (pbk. : alk. paper)

1. Mammoth Cave (Ky.)--History--19th century. 2. Mammoth
Cave (Ky.)--Description and travel. 3. Mammoth Cave Region
(Ky.)--History--19th century. 4. Mammoth Cave Region (Ky.)--
Description and travel. 5. Tourism--Kentucky--Mammoth Cave
Region--History--19th century. 6. Tourists--Kentucky--Mammoth
Cave Region--History--19th century. I. Title.

F457.M2O44 2010
976.9'754--dc22

2010012533

Published by CAVE BOOKS
4700 Amberwood Drive
Dayton, Ohio 45424-4602
http://www.cavebooks.com

CAVE BOOKS is the publications affiliate of the Cave Research
Foundation

Publisher: Roger McClure
Editor: Paul Steward, Tom Rea
Layout: Tom Rea, Greyhound Press
Cover Graphic Design: Gary Berdeaux
Front Cover drawing: Mammoth Dome
Back Cover drawing: Gothic Avenue

Printed in the United States of America

Table of Contents

1

Acknowledgements

Many thanks to everyone who helped make *Mammoth Cave by Lantern Light* possible. Mammoth Cave aficionados Roger Brucker, Rick Olson, and Elizabeth Winkler proof read the manuscript. Sandra L. Staebell and other staff members at Western Kentucky University's Kentucky Library provided historic illustrations of Mammoth Cave. National Park ranger Dave Sholar shared his collection of historic prints. Artist Bonnie Curnock shared her painting of nineteenth century guide Stephen Bishop. Caver/author/editor Paul Steward from Cave Books and Tom Rea from Greyhound Press took the time to edit the manuscript.

A Crystal Palace Underground
An Introduction

In 1815, the owners of a mammoth-size saltpeter cave in Kentucky were faced with a business problem. The War of 1812 had just ended in a draw between the United States and Great Britain. Most Americans considered the end of the war to be good news, but for the cave's owners, Charles Wilkins and Hyman Gratz, it meant less demand for saltpeter (the main ingredient in black gunpowder), therefore less money to be made from mining in their cave. They had invested money in the cave, so they needed to devise a new underground money-making scheme. Their new plan must have sounded crazy at the time—they would charge people one dollar to see the big, dark, cold, Mammoth Cave.

Paying to go on a cave tour is not far-fetched today, but in the early 1800s, a dollar was a lot of money. Only the wealthy could afford to travel, and Kentucky was the western frontier—a tough place to reach, even for the rich. But Wilkins and Gratz's crazy plan worked. People traveled a long way over rough country, shelled out their money, traipsed by lantern light through rough cave—and loved it.

Mammoth Cave's first tourists arrived in a trickle, but people who visited the cave wrote books and articles about it, and travelers told friends back home about their underground adventures, making the cave famous. Nineteenth century travelers felt Mammoth Cave was on the must-see list of American sites; they compared it to other famous spectacular attractions: natural and man-made, new world and old. In 1857, a European traveler wrote, "If, in his old age, the mental vigor of an American traveler should weaken, and even if he has completely forgotten all that he has seen in this land, still inscribed indelibly on the empty tables of his memory will be two events: when he first caught sight of Niagara Falls, and when he descended into Mammoth Cave."[1] Some descriptions were quite extravagant. In 1855, the famous travel writer Bayard Taylor asked, "What are the galleries of the Vatican, the Louvre, Versailles, and the crystal palaces of London and Paris to this gigantic vault hewn in the living rock?"[2]

Let's explore this underground "crystal palace" the way nineteenth century visitors did.

The Rough Road to Mammoth Cave

As today's travelers drive down the road toward Mammoth Cave, they consult road signs, maps, GPS, the trip odometer, and convenience store cashiers for directions. With all that help, it might seem impossible to miss the road to the cave. Nevertheless, some people do miss it. In the nineteenth century, finding the way was even harder. Frederick Hall wrote this description of his 1838 search for Mammoth Cave.

> The road was nothing but a horse-path, to be kept by means of marked trees. A colored boy, at his master's bidding, accompanied me two miles, and then said, "I'll go back, sir, now; the path is plain; if you look well to the blazed trees, you can't get wrong." Blazed, blazed, said I, that is a new word, or rather, a use of it, to which my ears have not been accustomed: what does it mean, boy? "It means blazed, sir, I don't know nothing more about it. The trees are blazed, but you must look sharp." Does it mean marked? "Mighty near, sir." He left me, and I moved forward, guideless, two miles farther, and then, perchance, met an old woman, of thick lips and ebony hue, of whom I inquired the way to the Mammoth Cave. "You can't miss it, sir, for a heap of strangers were along here last week." But I did miss it.[3]

In those days, most roads were little more than dirt trails—dusty in the summer, muddy in the winter. To encourage business, the manager of Mammoth Cave obtained a court order to open the first public highway to the cave in 1836; it ran about 8 miles from Bell's Tavern in the community of Three Forks (now called Park City)[4]. Though the public road was probably an improvement, it was still rough, even by nineteenth century standards. Travelers in the 1800s wrote that the ride from Bell's Tavern to the cave was, "horrible"[5] and "two hours jolting in a buggy over a most uncomfortable road."[6]

Bell's Tavern was a logical starting point for a road to Mammoth Cave. Many travelers destined for the cave stopped at Bell's for food, drink, and a night's rest before continuing. Today, a tavern is a place to drink beer and wine, but in the 1800s and earlier, taverns provided not only alcohol, but food, lodging, information, and more. They often served as public meeting houses (hence the name "pub") where friends gathered to exchange news and gossip, businessmen made deals, and politicians discussed politics.

William Bell, the tavern keeper, lived his whole life near Mammoth Cave and served many customers bound for the cave, yet he had no interest in seeing it himself. In 1851, a cave visitor wrote that Bell was ...

> ... a rather whimsical but thoroughly obliging, hospitable, and, I believe, excellent old gentleman, at whose hotel we were staying on our way to and from the Mammoth Cave. Singularly enough, he has lived for nearly half a century within a few miles of the cavern, but never has visited it. "Time enough," he growled, in a voice that might have sounded from the subterranean depths of the cave itself, and would have rumbled at Echo River, like a discharge of Satanic artillery, "Time enough to go underground when I'm dead," and we almost agreed with him, after we had all gone a-caving, and come back feeling so subterranically sepulchral, and with such a dreary antediluvian fossil-like sensation, perfectly convinced of the hollowness of the world in general, and of Kentucky in particular. Indeed, we rather envied Mr. Bell, his superficial views and his never having been buried alive, or trodden underfoot by half a quarter of the inhabitants of the state.[7]

One story (probably more tall-tale than fact) tells of the night when the only guest at Bell's Tavern was a young lawyer. He visited with Mr. Bell and Bell's niece in the parlor, talking about the news of the day—a murder had been committed in southern Kentucky and authorities believed the escaped killer was heading their way. The niece, excited at the prospect of a killer lurking nearby, suggested they search the tavern. Near the end of their search, the three entered the last room. The murderer, who had been hiding there all day, leapt from behind the door and ran. Frightened, the niece fainted, as any proper Victorian lady would have done under the circumstances. She dropped her lamp on the bed, which burst into flames, burning Bell's Tavern to the ground.[8]

Bell's Tavern did burn down in the late 1850s. Construction of a new tavern began, but, alas, the Civil War brought construction to a halt. The stone walls of what the Bell family hoped would become a magnificent new Bell's Tavern are still standing, unfinished in Park City. The site is on the National Register of Historic Places.

Bear Wallow Tavern was another haven for weary travelers near Mammoth Cave. The tavern and the community were named after a muddy depression where animals liked to roll in the mud. A sign with a picture of a black bear above the word "WALLOW" stood in front of the tavern to welcome guests.[9] An 1852 traveler wrote of his unpleasant arrival but over-all pleasant stay at Bear Wallow Tavern.

> I came to the tavern, where I was violently set upon by two dogs—and, after a fight with sticks and stones for 15 minutes, succeeded in rousing a black girl from her sleep, and gaining admittance and a bed. Spite of the dog-welcome given to the traveler, Bearwallow [sic] Tavern is liberally and kindly kept. A Negro came into my room in the morning with a large tub of water, (a bathing luxury not common even in more frequented places,) the breakfast set for me alone would have fed twenty persons, and the society of the landlady and her head man was thrown in. Charge for lodging, bath, breakfast, and the conversation of two very agreeable persons, only fifty cents.[10]

Even though Bear Wallow Tavern was not as popular as Bell's Tavern, it did attract famous customers. Showman P.T. Barnum and Jenny Lind, the nineteenth century's most famous singer, were spotted there when Lind toured America with Barnum. The Confederate Secretary of War, General John Breckenridge, visited at Bear Wallow. Peter Cooper, who invented the "Tom Thumb," the first steam locomotive built in the United States, and the gelatin recipe that later evolved into Jell-O, graced the tavern with his presence. Prominent politicians who stopped in at Bear Wallow include Kentucky governor Beriah Magoffin, who declared Kentucky neutral during the Civil War; John J. Crittenden, another Kentucky governor and a senator for whom the town of Crittenden, Kentucky, was named; Ohio governor Tom Corwin; Tennessee governor Isham G. Harris; congressman Aaron Harding; and the famous emancipationist, publisher, and Minister to Russia, Cassius M. Clay.

With the start of the Civil War, fewer travelers arrived at Bear Wallow Tavern, causing it to close in 1862. What remained of the grand old building burned down in 1914.[11]

Some people traveled to the cave in private carriages, but many arrived by stagecoach from Cave City or Three Forks. According to an 1879 newspaper article, the first local stagecoach service to Mammoth Cave started in 1833, when "... the road to the Cave was literally nothing more than an ox-path, along which he [the stage driver] was obliged to slowly feel his way at considerable risk to himself and passengers."[12] In 1885, Albert Tissandier, a French artist and balloonist, wrote about the rough, but fun, stagecoach trip in his journal.

> Only the victims themselves can believe the number of dreadful bumps, holes, and ruts in the road. But in the United States it is necessary to accustom ones self to this kind of voyage and the only thing to do is to laugh heartily. The American ladies who were the ornaments of our little excursion were the first to give us the signal. They were delighted, and the more the wagon shook, the happier they seemed. We tried to ease the shocks and bumps by giving them our shawls and blankets, but they only burst out laughing again.[13]

Today, it takes about 15 minutes to drive from nearby Park City (formerly Three Forks) to Mammoth Cave. In the 1800s, the 8-mile stage trip took two hours. Worse yet was the 90-mile trip from Louisville, "A tedious and fatiguing stage-coach journey of 18 hours." according to an 1855 traveler.

Travel was not only time consuming, but expensive. A school teacher on an excursion to the cave in 1868 wrote that the 18-mile round trip to and from Cave City cost $2.50.[14] Once you adjust for inflation and average wages for the time, $2.50 equals about $280 in 2007.[15] In 1854, John Ward wrote in his diary, "We paid $16.00 for our seats ..." on the stage from Louisville to Mammoth Cave.[16] It is unclear whether that was per ticket, or $16 for him and two companions; either way it was an expensive trip, $16 in 1868 would be about $1,792 in modern money. An 1887 traveler warned other tourists, "What a good cave tourist needs are the following: good shoes—and money, second: persistence—and money, third: not very good clothes—and money, and fourth: incidentally, quite a bit of money."[17]

Nineteenth century stagecoaches had no radios, no movies, and no coffee service. The bumpy roads probably made reading difficult, so travelers amused themselves by looking at the scenery and chatting with fellow passengers. Stage drivers sometimes joined in the talk and shared their opinions on Mammoth Cave. John Ward wrote, "Our driver said that the Mammoth Cave was a great humbug, only a great hole in the ground, with a lot of incrustations!"[18] Some stage drivers thought more highly of the cave. H.C. Hovey, who wrote several books about Mammoth Cave in the late 1800s, asked his driver, Jehu, if Mammoth Cave had any equals.

> "No, siree", responded Jehu, with a crack of the whip that made the leaders prance, "I reckon it's wuth fifty sich holes in the groun'. What's your notion about it, Judge?" "I have visited the chief caverns of the West," replied the judge, "and in my opinion, going from any one of them to Mammoth Cave is like exchanging a log cabin for a palace!"[19]

Most of the time, the ride was uneventful. But one September day in 1880, the passengers got more excitement than they wanted. The stagecoach "Florida" (some coaches had names, like ships) was rolling away from Mammoth Cave toward Cave City on its 5:00 P.M. run when a passenger said, "I see two men on the road behind us taking a drink out of a bottle." The men jumped on their horses, caught up to the stage, drew a gun, and told the driver to stop near the Little Hope Baptist Church and cemetery.* Everyone was ordered out of the coach except an elderly gentleman named R.H. (called Judge by his friends) Rowntree and his daughter Lizzie. Realizing they were about to be robbed, Lizzie stashed her three rings under the seat cushion, but one of the robbers turned over the cushion and found them. The robber stole $30.00, an engraved gold watch and a watch key from Judge Rowntree. The same robber, who appeared to be the boss, ordered everyone outside the coach to hand over their valuables. The amount of money and jewelry that were thrown onto the pile apparently did not meet the robber's expectations because he shouted, "Now I am going to search you in a moment, and if I find a dollar on any of you I will blow his [your] brains out." More valuables were handed over.

Aside from stealing the passenger's valuables and threatening to kill them, the robbers were polite. They claimed they were not robbers by profession, but moonshiners who needed the money to escape the revenuers, and that they would write down everyone's name and address so they could pay them back later. When the head robber learned where the Rowntrees were from, he covered his face with his bandanna and claimed to know some Rowntrees. He asked Lizzie if

---

* "Little Hope" isn't an encouraging name for a church or a cemetery, but the church was not named for the lack of hope for the congregation's afterlife, but for the steep saddle the church was built in. In rainy weather, a wagon or buggy had little hope of getting up the muddy hills. The church is gone, but the cemetery is still there. The modern paved road makes for an easy drive today.

she knew the Gray girls of Lebanon. When she said she did, he said "So do I, and they are nice girls. Give them my regards when you see them, and tell them that I will make this right some day." The robber than announced, "As I have done pretty well, I feel that I ought to treat," and passed around a bottle of whiskey (which they had stolen from another stagecoach heading toward the cave earlier that day) and ordered all the men to have a drink. To show what kind fellows they were, the robbers returned the passengers' railroad tickets and rode away.[20]

According to one story, the stage robbers did not make out as well as they could have. That morning, Mammoth Cave's owner, Julia Jesup, had $6,000 to send to the bank. She was afraid to send the money by stage; maybe she had read or heard of recent robberies nearby. Instead, Miss Jesup wrapped the money in six bundles of $1,000 each and had an employee named Jim Brown take the money to town, riding through the woods on horseback. By keeping off of the road, Mr. Brown avoided the robbers and got the money to the bank.[21]

When word of the Mammoth Cave stage robbery spread, some local folks suspected the head robber was Thomas J. Hunt, a former school teacher turned coal miner and part-time robber. Several people said they had seen him near the cave on the day of the robbery. Hunt was arrested and brought to nearby Cave City for the victims to identify. The stagecoach drivers and Rowntree did not recognize him, but another passenger swore Hunt was one of the robbers. Hunt had not been at work at the coal mine on the day of the robbery, he had no alibi, he could not post the $800 bail, and there were no other suspects. The judges decided they had enough evidence to indict Hunt for robbery on March 18, 1881.

Meanwhile, Rowntree had heard that Clarence Hite, a member of the infamous James gang, had been captured, tried, and imprisoned for train robbery in the Missouri State Penitentiary. Doubting that Hunt was the man who had stolen his watch and his daughter's rings, Rowntree wondered if the robbers could have been the famous outlaws Frank and Jesse James. He wrote to the prison warden in Missouri and asked him to question Hite about the Mammoth Cave robberies.

After a year in the Glasgow jail, Hunt went to trial and pleaded not guilty. Rowntree and several other witnesses continued to declare that Hunt was not one of the robbers. But Hunt insulted the witnesses who testified against him, did not cooperate with the prosecuting attorney, and was accused of having a "sullen demeanor," making him unpopular with the jury. He was found guilty and sentenced to three years in prison.

Right after the trial, Rowntree received a letter from the warden in Missouri. When questioned, Hite told the warden that Jesse James and fellow gang member Bill Ryan robbed the Mammoth Cave stagecoaches. Two days later, on April 3, 1882, Jesse James was shot and killed in St. Joseph, Missouri. In Jesse's pocket was Rowntree's engraved gold watch. Since the jig was up, Ryan soon admitted that he and James robbed the Mammoth Cave stages, and Jesse had been the spokesman.

With the real robbers dead or in jail, Thomas Hunt was eventually released. After comparing photos of Hunt and James, Rowntree and other witnesses admitted they looked a lot alike. Rowntree got his watch back, but with a price. Enos Craig, the Marshall who found the watch in Jesse James' pocket, believed finders keepers, losers weepers and demanded $30 for it. Jesse's widow, Zerelda James, refused to return the watch's gold key and Lizzie Rowntree's diamond ring, though she mailed back Lizzie's gold ring.

Rowntree enjoyed showing off his recovered watch; being stolen by Jesse James gave it celebrity status. The watch was eventually donated to The Filson Club, a historical society in Louisville, Kentucky. In 1967, the watch was stolen again, never to be recovered.[22]

The Louisville & Nashville (L&N) Railroad began rail service to Cave City in 1858.[23] Travelers destined for Mammoth Cave could ride in modern (at the time) luxury for most of their trip and only had to endure the bumpy stage ride for the last few miles.

Cave area stagecoach drivers lost their job security when the Mammoth Cave Railroad, a 9-mile spur off of the L&N Railroad, opened for business in 1886, allowing travelers to go all the way to the cave by rail. Passengers got off of the L&N train in the town of Glasgow Junction[24] and boarded a smaller train bound for the cave.

The Mammoth Cave Railroad engines were "dummies." This is not an insult to their locomotive intellect; it refers to their small size and design. Dummies were usually used on city street railways; the Mammoth Cave Railroad engines all had former lives pulling streetcars. The little dummies were not as big as their brethren that pulled trains for long distances on the L&N Railroad, but they were strong enough to get the job done. One engine was affectionately named "Hercules," after the legendary strongman from Greek mythology.

The Mammoth Cave Railroad's main job was carrying tourists to Mammoth Cave for $2.00 a ticket, but the train also carried freight and mail. Local people could hitch a free ride. An article in the Louisville *Courier-Journal* mentioned the engineer's helpfulness and his limits.

Pat Moran was the cussing, cocky engineer on "Hercules," and his fireman was Pete Charlet. Housewives along the line used to depend on Moran and Charlet to fetch them spools of thread, etc., on their run from Glasgow Junction. Homefolks rode the train free of charge, but Pat drew the line at stopping too often to let children on. But they'd get back at him on the return trip by soaping the rails and causing Hercules to stall. In these frequent emergencies, passengers had to get out and push. Pat's temper was so brittle he bit his pipe stem in two every time a cow got on the track in front of Hercules.

Hercules' days were numbered when the first automobile arrived at Mammoth Cave in 1904. In spite of a large deficit, the little trains kept chugging to the cave until 1929, when Hercules and the other dummies were replaced by a rail bus—a Ford bus fitted with wheels that could run on the railroad tracks. In 1931, the Mammoth Cave Railroad completely folded.[24] Today, part of the railroad route is a bicycle trail. A Mammoth Cave Railroad engine and a passenger car are on display between the Mammoth Cave Hotel and the campground—a reminder of the days of transition between the horse and the automobile.

Though most travel to Mammoth Cave was over land, some people made part of the trip by boat. Riverboat travel could range from rough to luxurious, depending on how much you were willing to pay.

In the late 1860s, a young man named Ralph Seymour Thompson set out with a band of friends to seek adventure at Mammoth Cave. The group's quest for adventure (and lack of cash) drove them to buy

Hercules was one of the engines on the Mammoth Cave Railroad.

deck passage (the cheap tickets) on a boat going from Bowling Green, Kentucky, to Evansville, Indiana, on their trip home. Thompson imagined there would be "a spice of romance about the idea of deck passage" but he had different feelings when the trip was over. In his book, *The Sucker's Visit to the Mammoth Cave*, he wrote:

But what about deck passage? Well, the result of my experience might be summed up in one word of advice to any other young man who has any idea of taking deck passage for the romance of the thing:

DON'T!

If being kicked and cuffed about like a dog is romantic, then deck passage is romantic; yes, extremely so.

... If having to steal off out of sight and snatch a mouthful to eat, as you can get a chance, and bribe the cook to boil your coffee, is romantic, then there is an abundance of romance about deck passage on a steamboat.

... Yes, if all these things are romance, then this trip was the most romantic episode of our lives. But I can't stand so much romance—not of this kind.[25]

The Mammoth Cave Hotel

Like twenty-first century Mammoth Cave visitors, nineteenth century travelers could get food and rest at the Mammoth Cave Hotel. The hotel that today's visitors see was built in 1963, but some visitors remember childhood trips to the old hotel built in 1926. An even older hotel served guests in the 1800s.

The first Mammoth Cave Hotel had a humble beginning as a log cabin built for Archibald Miller, a manager of the Mammoth Cave saltpeter mining operation from 1811 and 1812. When the cave went from being a saltpeter mine to a tourist attraction, the cabin evolved into a full-fledged hotel. A stable, fences, cottages, and new rooms were built in the late 1830s.[26]

John Croghan, a doctor from Louisville, Kentucky, bought Mammoth Cave and the hotel in 1837 and made many improvements. His heirs owned the cave until it was purchased to become a national park in 1925. In an 1839 letter to Archibald Miller, Dr. Croghan mentioned the possibility of creating a hotel inside Mammoth Cave.

> Here I remarked to one of the guides, Mr. Miller, you ought to have an Hotel, well supplied with refreshments of all kinds, chambers on one side for the ladies and the other for gentlemen, a handsomely furnished parlor, reading room and dining room, and all brilliantly illuminated. The idea of such an establishment was novel to him, its appropriateness immediately flashed upon his mind, and he wondered that such a thing had never been thought of before, for said he "I would charge a little higher and make three times as much from the Tavern within as that above ground." ... An Hotel under ground at the distance of 5 or 6 miles, and a stage to convey passengers thereto, is itself so unique, that, I think uncommon with all whom I have heard speak as the subject, it would be a means of increasing greatly the number of visitors.[27]

With the cave's constant temperature near 54 degrees Fahrenheit, it would have been the only air conditioned hotel in the nineteenth century. But the underground hotel never came to be. An old joke says potential customers would have been scared by the possible name for the underground hotel—the Mammoth Cave Inn.

The Mammoth Cave Hotel was comfortable, but by some travelers' standards, far from fancy. An 1838 traveler wrote, "The Cave-House is one of the commonest, one-story, frame dwellings, much out of repair ..."[28] A more satisfied visitor wrote in 1853:

> The cave Hotel is a large building or rather buildings not to be admired for their beauty, elegance, or costliness, but are well adapted to the comfort and convenience of visitors.
>
> The Proprietor of the Hotel is one of the most accommodating gentlemanly men that may be met with anywhere. He spares no pains in trying to render visitors easy and comfortable. There is no information relative to the Cave which he is not as ready, as free to give, as you are to receive. His table is spread with plenty of all that is palatable and inviting to the appetite.[29]

Mammoth Cave's fame brought the hotel plenty of customers. In 1859, a visitor said the hotel was "splendid" and people "flock here from Calcutta and China and every part of Europe and America."[30]

During the Civil War from 1861 to 1865, the cave continued to operate as a tourist attraction. Kentucky was a neutral border state, with Union and Confederate supporters. Both Union and Confederate soldiers passing through stopped to enjoy a peaceful stay at the hotel and a cave tour. But one visit from Confederate soldiers was not recreational. J.R. Underwood, a trustee of Mammoth Cave Estate, wrote in the "Report of affairs at the 'Mammoth Cave' for the year 1861," that the hotel manager, Mr. Owsley, was told to remove the valuables from the hotel because Confederate soldiers were on their way to burn it down. Many valuables were stashed in the cave for safe keeping. Books, registers, and receipts were put in an iron safe and taken out in the yard. The hiding places did not work. Underwood wrote:

> ... the confederate troops commenced depredations upon the property, taking beds, blankets, and every thing they could apply to their use. They destroyed a great portion of the furniture in mere wantonness, which they could not remove and use. After doing

that they left the premises without burning the houses.[31]

A Texas Ranger known only as Frank wrote about the raid in a letter to his wife.

> Our present camp being but 10 miles from Mammoth Cave some of the boys rode over there yesterday and found the Hotel closed and all the valuables carried two or three miles into the Cave. The proprietor is a Union Man and our men helped themselves freely to choice liquors, cutlery, bedding, cooking utensils, etc. ...[32]

An English traveler visiting in the mid-1860s commented on the war, the raid, and his hotel bed.

> But evil days had come upon the house, for the disturbed state of the district had thinned the stream of visitors, and put an end to all its gay doings. Then, some time ago, the Confederates swooped down upon the place, for Mr. Owsley, the proprietor, had remained loyal; they ordered him to take out all his furniture, telling him that they were going to burn down the house. So he took out all his things, and placed them for shelter in the mouth of the cave; no sooner had he done which, than the Confederates took the things and spared the house. So this accounts for the beds being the hardest I ever slept upon in all my life.[33]

It took a while for the Mammoth Cave Hotel to recover from the Civil War. When Dr. William Stump Forwood visited the cave around 1870, he mentioned that the hotel was run-down, but he was still impressed. In *An Historical and Descriptive Narrative of the Mammoth Cave of Kentucky* he wrote:

> ... the proprietors suffered so severely from the entire loss of business during those four or five gloomy years, it has not yet been rebuilt Other marks of dilapidation are also apparent, from the same cause; but as the return-tide of visitors begins to flow, with its attendant prosperity, evidences of restoration are visible.
> ... There are not many summer resorts where an individual or a family can pass a few weeks more pleasantly or more profitably than at the Mammoth Cave Hotel. Here are to be found all the advantages of a first-class watering-place hotel, with the addition

19

Hotel visitors danced The Mammoth Cave Schottisch in the ballroom.
A schottisch is a Scottish dance with music similar to a polka.

of fine country scenery, and daily opportunities of observing Nature's great subterranean wonder.[34]

Things eventually improved. The hotel offered enough activities in addition to cave tours that some guests were enticed to stay for extended periods. An 1872 newspaper advertised:

The Mammoth Cave Hotel, newly fitted and furnished, is first-class in every respect. Amusements of every kind, splendid dancing hall, music and dancing free; billiards, croquet, target practice, base ball, etc. Fine fishing, boating, and hunting near the hotel.

RATES: Per day, first two days, $3.50; after first two days, $2.50; per week, $17.50; per month, $50.[35]

Horace Hovey, a nineteenth century cave enthusiast who visited and wrote about many American caves, wrote about the grand welcome and other pleasantries of his stay at the hotel in 1882.

A bugle flourish heralds the arrival of passengers, and brings around the coach a throng of guests expecting friends, or curious to see strangers, and plenty of Negro servants offering to take care of luggage.

The hotel register shows an aggregate of from 2,000 to 3,000 visitors a year. Many of these come from the North, and a few from various parts of Europe, drawn by their curiosity to behold this far-famed locality. The majority, however, are from Louisville, Nashville, Memphis, New Orleans, and other cities of the Sunny South; and he who wishes to meet the best types of southern society, will be sure of finding them here.

... Extensive gardens supply the hotel with fresh vegetables of every kind, and the table is furnished amply with whatever the season and the market may afford.

... a more airy, delightful place can not be found in the State of Kentucky! ... How many thousands of tourists, savants, and

The Mammoth Cave Hotel in 1895.

lovers have here strolled in the moonlight! At 11:00 P.M. the band left the ball-room for the veranda, and, according to their custom, gave the signal for retiring by playing "Home, sweet home;" and the next morning, at six, the same musicians awoke us by playing "Dixie"—that tune dear to every Southern heart![36]

Not everyone was impressed with the post-war quality of the hotel. French artist Albert Tissandier wrote in his 1885 journal that his hotel room was, "almost a monk's cell. ... Provisions are not easily obtained at Mammoth Cave, consequently the food here is simple."[37]

Another visitor wrote in 1887 that the music at the hotel was "atrocious" and the weedy flowerbeds and paths attested to "departed splendor."[38]

William P. Kendrick was one of the old Mammoth Cave Hotel's last guests. In 1936, he wrote a letter to the Louisville *Courier-Journal* about his December 9, 1916, stay at the hotel:

> About 1:00 A.M. we were awakened by a man shouting and running up and down the porches and knocking upon all the doors. We naturally thought that he was drunk and was playing a joke on us, but opening our eyes we found that the entire dining hall was ablaze, it being only two or three rooms away from ours.

The hotel burned to the ground that night. Nearly a decade later, the second Mammoth Cave Hotel was completed.

Into the Cave

Early Mammoth Cave visitors enjoyed socializing, dancing, and listening to music above ground, but the main reason they came was to see the world's most famous cave.

Today, children are big fans of the cave, but in the 1800s, cave tours were apparently only for adults. Remembering her 1872 visit, a woman wrote, "My governess and my sister went into the cave. They left me at the hotel, as I was too small to make the trip."[39]

Modern Mammoth Cave visitors have many tours to choose from, but in the 1800s there were just two; the Short Route, which took about 4 hours,[40] and the Long Route which took 9 to 12 hours.[41] If travelers had the time, energy, and money to see more of the cave, they could hire a guide to take them into passages off the main tour routes.[42]

If visitors wanted to spare their clothes from the cave's dirt and avoid tripping over long skirts, they could rent special clothes for the trip. "How any lady could have accomplished that descent, notwithstanding the bloomer costume they always wear in the caves, I could not understand,"[43] an 1860 visitor commented after a steep climb. Women's fashion in particular—long dresses, high button shoes, petticoats, and corsets—were not the best attire for scrambling over rocky trails in a dark cave.

In spite of the difficulties of getting around the cave in typical 1800s clothes, some people chose not to pay the 50 cents[44] to one dollar to rent a costume.[45] At least one woman regretted her decision to wear her normal clothes on a cave trip—her abandoned corset is still lying in the dirt in a steep, rocky passage called the Corkscrew; she apparently decided breathing and climbing were more important than fashion.

In 1854, Charles C. Jones described colorful cave costumes in a letter to his parents. He did not say whether the costumes the cave visitors wore were rented from the hotel or purchased beforehand, but the outfits were not their normal clothes.

The ladies were all dressed in bloomer costume ... yellow flannel, tastefully trimmed with black velvet, the upper garments gracefully confined around the waist by a sash, and wearing light blue turbans with black plumes upon the head. The costume was really pretty, and Turkish in appearance. ... George Helm and myself wore scarlet flannel coats, with collars, pocket flaps, and edges lined and trimmed with black cotton velvet. Our pants were of light green color of the same material ... small caps completed our fanciful costume. The ladies are compelled to adopt this mode of dress as that best adapted to promote that freedom of action which is indispensable among the rocks and uneven surfaces of this subterranean region. You may readily imagine the fantastic appearance presented by some thirty tourists, each one arrayed in garments such as his or her taste may suggest as most becoming the occasion.[46]

This sketch of dapper cave visitors was published in an 1871 issue of the magazine Every Saturday. Notice that the lanterns are for holding candles, not burning oil.

Once properly attired, the tour group trekked down the hill to the Historic Entrance, at the time the only known entrance to Mammoth Cave (today we know of 26 entrances). This natural entrance cuts into the earth beneath a hill that hides it from eager visitors' eyes as they approach from above. Upon arrival, visitors not only see the cave, but feel its cool breath blowing out. An 1852 traveler called the entrance "a huge cavernous arch, filled in with immense stones, as if giants had piled them there, to imprison a conquered demon."[47] Along with awe and curiosity, the dark, gaping hole can inspire fear. An 1887 visitor commented, "Here a peculiar, unnameable feeling, a 'quiet horror' comes over a person, and it has gripped many a tourist to such an extent that he turned around at the entrance and returned home without having accomplished his purpose."[48] This uneasy feeling continued to grip some visitors as they descended into the first passage, called the Narrows. The famous writer Robert Montgomery Bird wrote about the passage in 1838:

> ... we find ourselves at the Narrows. ... Here, if the nervous visitor has not been appalled at the entrance, he will perhaps be dismayed by the furious blast rushing like a winter tempest through the door. Its strength is indeed astonishing. It deprives him of breath, and, what is worse, of light; the torches are blown out; they are relighted and again extinguished: we must grope our way through in the dark, and trust to flint and steel.[49]

Saltpeter miners used bored out logs to pipe water into the cave and saltpeter out.

The Narrows opens into a large chamber called the Rotunda. The saltpeter mining equipment from the mining operation that was abandoned in 1816 still sits there today. Cave visitors in the early 1800s may have thought of the wooden pipes, vats, and pumps as old junk that no one bothered to clean up. As time passed, the saltpeter works rose in status from trash to precious historic artifacts. Mid-to-late 1800s visitors often mentioned seeing not only the old mining equipment but also wheel tracks and hoof prints from ox-drawn carts that hauled dirt. They also saw corncobs that were used to feed the oxen. Guides gave the corncobs to visitors as souvenirs. When the corncobs from the mining operation ran low, the guides brought a fresh supply of cobs into the cave to insure souvenirs for everyone.[50]

The Historic Entrance was the only known way into the cave in the 1800s. Today, there are 26 known entrances.

The Rotunda divides into two immense passages. Their mammoth size inspired the cave's name. The right fork leads to Little Bat Avenue, Crevice Pit, and Mammoth Dome. Today, Mammoth Dome has electric lights and a tower that modern tourists ascend from the cave's lower levels. In the 1800s, there were no lights and no stairs—just a dark, gaping pit that meager lantern light could not penetrate. Like all things that are mysterious and unattainable, Crevice Pit made people curious. According to Ebenezer Meriam, who visited Mammoth Cave in 1813 during the saltpeter mining operation, Mammoth Cave's owner, Charles Wilkins, suspected more saltpeter was waiting to be mined at the bottom of Crevice Pit. Trying to get a look, Wilkins tied a lantern to a rope and lowered it down the pit. The rope caught on fire and the lantern crashed to the bottom. Wanting to retrieve his lantern and learn what was down there, Wilkins offered the generous reward of two dollars to any miner brave enough to go down Crevice Pit on a rope. A miner called Little Dave volunteered for the job. Little Dave was lowered down the pit with a torch in his hand, but he did not make it to the bottom. Frightened by the

The earliest cave tourists may have viewed the saltpeter vats in the Rotunda as junk from the mining operation, but by the mid 1800s the vats were regarded as historic artifacts

experience, he said that, "no sum could tempt him to try again for the lamp." The lantern remained at the bottom of Crevice Pit until the late 1830s, when cave guide Stephen Bishop discovered the pit from the bottom via lower cave passages. Being the first person to set foot in that part of the cave, Stephen was no doubt surprised to find a lantern there.[51]

Tours, then as now, went down the Rotunda's left fork, called Broadway, which leads to a chamber called the Methodist Church (or the Church). Many 1800s visitors wrote that their guides told them church services were formally held in the cave, but there are no first-hand accounts of anyone attending a regular church service in the cave. But there was at least one special church service held at the Methodist Church. The Reverend C. Foster wrote of his one-time experience preaching in the cave.

> Among the hundred or more guests, there were three clergymen. When Sabbath morning, August 1, 1852, came, it was suggested that the day could not be spent more pleasantly than by having divine service. The two elder preachers, absolutely refused, and the conducting of the service fell upon myself, then a young man, having just entered the ministry. One aged brother strongly advocated having service in the ballroom, for said he, "it has been

polluted by the devil for six nights in the week, and needs now, very badly, to be somewhat purified by prayer and praise." The majority of the visitors decided that services be held in the church, in the Mammoth Cave. ... It was a beautiful sight from the pulpit, never to be forgotten, to see in the distance that strange audience, marching in single file, each carrying a lamp in the right hand to guide the feet on the way to this strange house of prayer, where the worshippers had never worshipped before, and where in all probability they would never worship again.[52]

The saltpeter miners could only gaze down Mammoth Dome through Crevice Pit. By the mid 1800s, visitors could enter Mammoth Dome from the bottom, climb up a short distance and gaze up the shaft by lantern or torch light. Modern visitors walk all the way up on a steel tower.

Gothic Avenue was on the first tour route in the cave. It was one of the few areas nineteenth century visitors could see stalactites.

Beyond the Church is Gothic Avenue, which earned this name by the mid 1800s because the formations reminded people of Gothic architecture. Earlier visitors called it the Haunted Chambers. An 1810 newspaper article, the earliest known printed use of the name Mammoth Cave, mentions the Haunted Chambers:

> "We passed one very extraordinary room, it is so formed that a voice at the entrance pronouncing a word, is reverberated distinctly six times. ... The vulgar suppose this room to be haunted, from the reverberation of the voice. They suppose there were persons in the room mocking them when they spoke."[53]

In his 1838 book *Peter Pilgrim: or A Rambler's Recollections*, Robert Montgomery Bird told another tale of the origin of the name Haunted Chambers. A saltpeter miner who was unfamiliar with the cave went down the passage alone. Afraid he was lost, the miner panicked, ran in terror, and tripped, putting out his light. Alone in the dark, he thought the worst:

> "... the poor fellow's frenzy increased; he felt himself a doomed man, he thought his terrible situation was a judgment imposed on him for his wickedness: nay he even believed, at last, that he was no longer an inhabitant of the earth—that he had been translated, even in the body, to the place of torment—in other words, that he was in hell."

When his fellow miners came searching for him, torches in hand, he mistook them for Satan's minions and ran away terrified. His companions caught up with him after he fell over a rock and eventually convinced him he was not in Hell, but in Mammoth Cave.[54]

Haunted Avenue (now Gothic Avenue) is also famous for some of the oldest English graffiti in the United States. Tourists' and guides' names, initials, dates, drawings of faces, stars, and hearts dating as far back as 1812 cover the walls and ceiling where nineteenth century visitors held up candles to smoke their mark on the cave. In the early-to-mid-1800s, writing on the cave was considered part of the fun, but not everyone approved of it. Many old-time cave tourists expressed disgust at the graffiti. A cave visitor wrote in a letter in 1853:

> It is a great pity that any visitor should display so little taste, as to mar the beauty of a natural curiosity simply to gratify a vain desire to leave his insignificant name, as a mark of his vanity, and want of good taste.[55]

This R.H. Munford signature from 1836 in Gothic Avenue may be Richard Henry Munford, the son of Richard Jones Munford, founder of the near-by town of Munfordville. Photo by Rick Olson.

In 1888, a law called *An Act to prevent trespass upon the Mammoth Cave in Kentucky* made graffiti or vandalism in the cave illegal; visitors who could not resist adding their names to the cave could be fined $50.[56]

When graffiti became taboo, travelers found other ways to leave their mark. From the late 1800s through the 1930s, people left their business and calling cards propped on the rocks or built stone

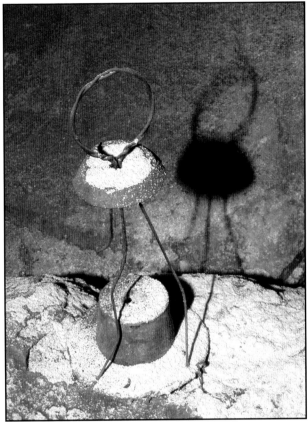

Guides and visitors left many lanterns in the cave in the 1800s.
This lantern, covered with mineral salts, still sits abandoned
near Devils Looking Glass in Mammoth Cave.
Photo by Rick Olson.

monuments. Visitors building a monument could leave a sign on it dedicating the monument to themselves, their hometown, state, college, or fraternal organization. Some people anticipated building monuments and had signs made before arriving at the cave. One monument bears a metal plaque that says A. Hohl Philadelphia, Penn 1887–1888. Members of the Dramatic Order Knights of Khorassan (a branch of The Order of Knights of Pythias, a fraternity dedicated to the cause of universal peace) left a shield they had made in advance. The calling cards are long gone, but many monuments, some with signs, some without, remain in Gothic Avenue and other passages.

Looking for shapes in the rocks was popular in the 1800s (and still is today). It is like gazing up at the clouds—with a little imagination you can see an assortment of bunnies, witches, or whatever else you fancy. A favorite place to use the imagination is on the ceiling above Broadway beyond Gothic Avenue. When modern visitors are asked what they see in this big, black splotch of gypsum, they answer, "a butterfly," "a dragon," or an assortment of other shapes, but they never guess the same image the 1800s cave guides thought it looked like. A German traveler described the shape in 1867:

> According to the guide's explanation it shows a giant, his wife and child. It seems to be evening. The giant after the day's work enjoys the joy of having a family. Like most giants he is a good house-wether. He is sitting on the ground, his long legs spreading out over half the ceiling of the cave. His wife, dearly going along with the humorous mood of her mighty husband, is sitting across him with spread out arms. The child (who is less perfect and could as well be a stone or a twin potato) is flying between both in the air. A darling picture of homely happiness.[57]

Other shapes that visitors saw in the rocky walls and ceiling include an anteater, a mammoth,[58] Napoleon on his horse, a catamount (cougar),[59] a flying Indian, a blacksmith's anvil, an aged man with a deer,[60] Barnum's fat girl,[61] a lion's head, and a human head with a wig called Lord Lyndhurst.[62] Some of these shapes were well known among the guides and still are occasionally shown today. Others were apparently favorites of particular guides and not widely shown—one person's anteater may have been another person's lion.

Star Chamber was, and still is, a popular place to use the imagination. Ralph Seymour Thompson wrote about his experience at Star Chamber in *The Sucker's Visit to the Mammoth Cave* in 1879:

> We raised our eyes, and behold we seemed to be beneath the dome of heaven! The arched roof above us, almost beyond our vision, was studded with twinkling stars innumerable. Light, fleecy clouds in places seemed to float across the sky hiding the stars from view. In one place a comet stretched its train. So complete was the delusion that it was difficult not to imagine that we had stayed in the cave till after night and had now found our way to the open air in some rock-bound ravine with nothing but rocks on either

side and the starry sky o'er head. And yet if we had found the outer world, it must have been a different world, for the stars were grouped in constellations we had never seen before. We had found a new heaven and a new earth.

Cave guides knew many tricks. They could use their lanterns to seemingly change the weather at Star Chamber:

"Sometimes," said Mat, [the guide] from his hiding place, "a storm comes up," and moving his lamps further away he caused a shadow black and threatening to gather in the far distance. Gradually it approached, like a frightful storm, o'erspread the sky, blotting out star after star, till it seemed about to envelope us in its inky folds.

Visitors crossed a bridge at a pool called the Dead Sea on their way to the rivers. This grand view of the Dead Sea existed only in the artist's imagination.

But the guides' favorite trick was to make the sun set and rise at Star Chamber. When Matt the guide disappeared with the lanterns into a side passage, Ralph and his companions feared they had been abandoned in the dark. But then:

"Look!" exclaimed Pete, "to the right, I see a glimmer of light."
"Crazy, already," said Nimrod, "you must have got clear turned

around. Don't you know that to the right is the way into the cave? Mat went the other way."

But we all turned and strained our eyes attempting to penetrate the darkness in the direction Pete had indicated, and sure enough, there was a gleam of light, one little star twinkled out, and then another. ... It seemed the glow of morning. In a moment more we heard Matt's voice very successfully imitating the crow of a rooster, and presently he himself appeared with the lamps in his hand.[63]

Most 1800s cave tours turned around at Star Chambers and headed for other passages, but sometimes guides continued with their groups down the huge passage of Broadway into parts of the cave less traveled. Trips into less familiar areas could lead to more adventure than planned. Just off of Broadway is a confusing room called Black Chambers. It is easy to get into, but tricky to get out of. Black Chambers is full of holes going nowhere; you have to find the right hole to get back to Broadway. In 1838, Robert Montgomery Bird wrote about two tourists and their disoriented guide who feared that rocks had fallen and sealed off the passage leading from Black Chambers to Broadway.

Here was a situation; and soon there was a scene. The young gentlemen became frantic; and, declaring they would sooner die on the spot than endure their horrible imprisonment longer, condemned to agonize out existence by inches, they drew their pistols—with which, like true American travelers, they were both well provided—resolving at once to end the catastrophe. The only difficulty was a question that occurred, whether each should do execution upon himself by blowing his own brains out, or whether, devoted to friendship even in death, each should do that office for the other. Fortunately, before the difficulty was settled, the guide stumbled upon one of the chimneys, and blood and gunpowder were both saved.[64]

There are many other 1800s stories about getting lost in the bewildering labyrinth of Mammoth Cave, though most involve people who wandered away from their guides, not guides who were lost. *A Guide Manual to the Mammoth Cave of Kentucky*, published in 1860, warned travelers of the dangers of straying from their trusted guides:

A person lost in the Mammoth Cave, without any hope of escape, would undoubtedly die in a very short time. This is the case, the history of those who have been lost in it would seem to prove.

Thus, on one occasion a gentleman wandered from his party, when by some accident his lamp was extinguished. In endeavoring to make his escape, he became alarmed, and finally insane. ...

In another instance a lady allowed her party to get so far in advance that their voices could no longer be heard, and in attempting to overtake them, fell and extinguished her lamp, when she became so terrified at her situation that she swooned, and when discovered a few minutes afterward, and restored, was found to be in a state of insanity, from which she did not recover for a number of years.

Not a year passes but the guides have to go in search of persons who have been foolhardy enough to leave their party, and who in every instance become speedily bewildered, and when discovered

By lantern light, Bottomless Pit looked deeper than a mere 105 feet; visitors believed it was whatever depth the guide said it was.

are in the act of crying, or at prayer. In such cases the guides are overpowered with kisses, embraces, and other demonstrations of gratitude.[65]

There are other accounts of the dire consequences of being lost in the cave. Stories tell of lost visitors being in a state of "temporary mental derangement,"[66] and when found, they "flung themselves sobbing on their saviors or sat speechless on the ground—insane."[67]

Being lost in the cave would be upsetting and scary, but I doubt it led to insanity. Stories of terrified people lost in the dark going mad probably worked better than simple warnings to keep people from wandering off in the cave.

In the early 1800s, tours remained in the cave's higher passages. They could only go so deep before they were cut off by Bottomless Pit—a mere 105 feet deep in reality, but by lantern light, it looks as deep as your imagination allows. Stephen Bishop, a guide who rose to legendary status in the mid 1800s, first crossed the pit in 1838. Story has it Stephen used a ladder or a pole as a makeshift bridge to take an adventurous visitor to passages previously unexplored. Soon after, a bridge was built and tours ventured across. Though the bridge was more stable than a ladder tossed across the pit, the trip

The Bridge of Sighs across Bottomless Pit was named after a bridge in Venice, Italy. The rickety wooden bridge has long since been replaced by stainless steel, but some modern visitors are still nervous crossing it.

over Bottomless Pit made some visitors nervous (and still does). Two 1850s visitors wrote:

> There is now a narrow bridge of two planks, with a little railing on each side; but it is impossible to sustain it by piers, travelers must pass over in the centre, one by one, and not touch the railing, lest they disturb the balance, and overturn the bridge.[68]
>
> Soon the old guide called "Bottomless Pit, be careful," and in a moment we were right over the awful cavern, down which we threw rock, and heard them down, down, down, till the sound died away .... My soul was horror-stricken when I gazed down into this dark and horrible vortex .... Some of our ladies grew faint at the very sight.[69] Lantern light did not do Bottomless Pit justice, so guides dropped flaming paper down it to show off its beauty and scariness.

After acrophobics have their excitement at Bottomless Pit, claustrophobes get their thrill at Fat Man's Misery—a narrow, winding passage that requires bending and twisting. Ladies who chose to wear their long skirts instead of renting a cave costume had extra trouble squeezing through. A guide in the 1850s joked, "Ladies, this road was made under the 'old constitution' before hoops came in fashion."[70] Watching less-than-skinny companions wiggle through Fat Man's Misery was considered good entertainment. Around 1850, a fat Englishman was described as looking :

> ... something like a huge pillow, of which the feathers had been displaced in one part and huddled up in another, which, in short, had shifted its cargo down! And that required shaking and putting it right. By degrees the metamorphosis ceased, and he shortly regained his natural shape.[71]

William Garvin, a long-time guide in the late 1800s, joked that he had to carry the fattest man that ever entered Fat Man's Misery through in sections, and showed visitors "where the rocks had to bend to let this jolly fat man through!"[72]

The descent into the deep, dark bowels of the earth made many people feel they had walked right into you-know-where. The hellishness of Mammoth Cave inspired many place names, like River Styx—named after the river that dead souls were ferried across to

Hades, the underworld of Greek mythology. Visitors hear Charon's Cascade, named for the ferryman on River Styx. One 1860s visitor may have felt he was bound for Hades as he boarded the boat at River Styx; he wrote, "The craft for it should have been huge coffins steered by skeletons and paddled by pale things in damp wormy shrouds."[73] Visitors who had the heebie-jeebies about the boat ride could cross River Styx on a bridge.

After crossing River Styx, another boat was waiting at Echo River. Modern visitors reach cave passages on the far side of the rivers via entrances blasted in the twentieth century, but in the 1800s, a long hike and a subterranean boat ride was the only way to get to the far reaches of the cave. Echo River could be scary; a traveler in 1852 said he felt "transplanted into some unearthly place inhabited by

Notice that the guide in the back of this group at Echo River is carrying a basket for an underground picnic.

demons."[74] But in spite (or maybe because) of their fear, most people had a good time on Echo River. Echoes can be heard in many places in Mammoth Cave, but those on Echo River are the best. Guides and visitors would sing, shout, fire guns, and blow horns to hear the sounds come back again and again. In the 1880s, cave guide Henry Bransford entertained visitors on Echo River.

> Here Henry stood up in the boat and sang with a full, melodious voice. ... Hardly had he ended, when there resounded out of the darkness in front of us, a full, extraordinarily splendid chord, which rolled in waves along the rocks, until it became lost again behind us in the darkness. The black man repeated his trick in the major and minor keys. We tourists could not get enough of listening. ...

Like Charon's boat, with its spirits of the dead, our boat glided along inaudibly, while the light of the lamps, which stood on the floor of the boat, allowed our own gigantic shadows to rush along on the smooth rock walls and disappear behind sharp promontories. Suddenly, Henry dropped his oar heavily on the edge of the boat. An indescribable crack as though the rocks were crashing together over us, and a thunder no longer earthly, was the echo's answer. That was one of Henry's favorite jokes, the effect of which he liked to read on the faces of his charges, pale with fright.[75]

A boat ride on Echo River about 360 feet underground.

Not all echoes were pleasant. Author Ralph Seymour Thompson wrote of his 1860s ride on Echo River:

> Now fairly out upon the waters, one of the young collegians took from its case a zither and played a few tunes. Music is always sweetest on the water, but here the roof and walls repeated the strains, till it seemed we were surrounded with music.
>
> "Now," said Nimrod, drawing out his Smith & Wesson revolver, "we'll try a little music of another kind," and he fired a couple of shots in quick succession. The low, overarching roof threw back the noise upon us with a crash that made us all dodge; then in a moment it seemed as if a hundred masked batteries had opened upon us; crash followed crash, till one would have imagined a naval engagement was in progress, then we could hear the roar rolling away in the distance; but in a minute it came rolling back upon us.[76]

Looking for and trying to catch eyeless cave fish was part of the

Washington Hall was a popular place for lunch. Horace Hovey, author of several books on Mammoth Cave, is on the far right.

fun on Echo River. "These little creatures are very treasured souvenirs with cave visitors and, as such, command enormous prices. A living example costs $3.00, while the dead ones cost $1.50," wrote a visitor who made the trip in 1887.[77]

As visitors got off the boat and climbed up the far shores of Echo River, they looked forward to reaching a chamber called Washington Hall—not because there was anything spectacular to see there but because it was a popular place to have lunch. A second guide often brought up the rear carrying food for the group. Judging from the number of chicken bones still in Washington Hall, chicken was a favorite meal. Food was washed down with plenty to drink. A member of the Illinois State Teachers' Association that visited the cave in 1869 wrote:

> Good water from a spring nearby was the beverage for us, although the broken bottles along the whole length of the cave told that the bar at the Cave Hotel had been doing a thriving business. The clerk at that bar said our company must be composed of ministers or teachers, as we did not drink anything.[78]

Just past Washington Hall is the gypsum-filled passage of

Cleveland's Cabinet. This area helped persuade people to devote the extra time, energy, and money it took to go on the Long Trip. Visitors admired beautiful "flowers" formed from gypsum—the mineral used to make drywall. An 1860s traveler wrote:

> This is the flower garden of the lower world: a conservatory of exotics. The rock grows a continuous and bountiful crop ... there is scarcely a flower known in the garden or conservatory that cannot be found reproduced in grace and beauty indescribable in this cabinet.[79]

Spectacular gypsum formations in Cleveland Avenue made walking 10 miles on the Long Trip worth the effort.

The gypsum formations were too tempting for many visitors to resist taking some home. An 1843 journal entry states:

> One curious clump of crystals after another was taken, until hands and pockets were filled. These were then deposited in a safe place and a fresh collection commenced. The different deposits were again culled over and after bringing with us as many as we could carry, we almost grieved to leave so much beauty behind.[80]

According to an article in an 1852 issue of *The International Magazine of Literature, Art, and Science*, the rules on taking gypsum changed.

Travelers have shown such wanton destructiveness in this great temple of Nature—mutilating beautiful columns, knocking off spar, and crushing delicate flowers—that the rules are now very strict. It is allowable to touch nothing, except the ornaments which have loosened and dropped by their own weight.[81]

This rule apparently was not always enforced. An 1863 visitor wrote:

In some portions of the cabinet there is not a space as large as your hand that is not covered with these beautiful, dazzling white plants, and the guides state that though thousands are destroyed every year by the brutal Yankee visitors, they have no fear of the stock being exhausted, as they are constantly growing and replacing those that have been destroyed. I do not believe this nonsense. The cabinet must have been infinitely more beautiful when first discovered, for the floor is literally thick with crumbled remains of the plants and flowers.[82]

After seeing the gypsum flowers at Cleveland's Cabinet, many tired visitors began the long trek back to the entrance. More energetic tourists continued to Rocky Mountain, where they would scramble up a big pile of limestone breakdown. Visitors' comments about the far end of the cave reveal Victorian attitudes toward women's capabilities. A visitor in 1887 wrote, "It is generally advisable for ladies not to hike farther along, since the next mile of the way is hardly passable for the tenderer sex."[83] An all-male tour group had a conversation on this subject with their guide, Mat Bransford, at Rocky Mountain in the 1860s.

"Mat," said I, "do ladies ever climb this mountain?"

"Oh yes, sir. Most every day during the season some ladies go over the mountain."

"Well, I don't see how they manage it. The girls at home generally claim to be exhausted after walking three quarters of a mile ..."

"Well," replied Mat, "there are almost always some young men along, and I never saw a young man so tired or so lazy he couldn't help a pretty girl up the Rocky Mountain."

"Humph!" said Nimrod, "How do the ugly girls do, Mat?"

"Well," replied Mat, "they most generally have to look out for themselves."[84]

The round trip to Rocky Mountain and back to the surface was about 10 miles, a respectable distance to walk and climb through twisty, rough, dark passages. The tiring journey made many tourists think they had traveled much further. Horace Hovey, who wrote several magazine articles and books on Mammoth Cave in the late 1800s, wrote, "It was gratifying to be assured by Tom [the cave guide] that we had probably tramped to and fro, in and out, about 100 miles. ..."[85] The exaggeration extended beyond how long the tour was to how long the entire cave was. Only about 30 miles of Mammoth Cave had been discovered by the late 1800s, but guides and visitors claimed the cave was 110,[86] 150,[87] 300,[88] or even 600 miles long.[89] Even though they were stretching the length way beyond what had actually been surveyed at the time, their wild exaggerations turned out to be not so wild. As of 2006, Mammoth Cave has been surveyed to be more than 365 miles long.

As tired visitors emerged from the cave, their senses perked up to take in every day sights, smells, and sounds that often go unnoticed. An 1860s visitor wrote:

> Those who have come out of the Cave in broad daylight say the effect is both unpleasant and peculiar. At first one is almost blinded: then the country has a strange, unnatural appearance. The lights and shadows strangely sharp and bright.
>
> But one thing we could not help but notice—the overpowering perfumes. The air seemed loaded with the scent of the earth, the flowers, the leaves, a thousand perfumes mingled, and produced, at first, a sense almost of suffocation.
>
> And then we seemed in a perfect babble of noises—the notes of the birds, of the tree frogs, the falling of the twigs and the leaves, seemed to echo and re-echo through the air in endless confusion.[90]

When travelers returned home with their stories of flower-shaped minerals, underground boat rides, giants tossing babies, and a starry sky in a cave, their accounts were often regarded as tall tales. A man who had visited the cave in the 1890s sat in a Chicago saloon after returning from his trip and told his drinking companions about how in Mammoth Cave the guide blew out the lanterns so the tour group could experience total darkness. When the guide reached for his matches to relight the lanterns, he realized he had lost them—causing the terrified party to sit in the dark listening to their hearts beat with fear for ten hours until a search party found them, said the traveling man. The bartender silently listened to what he thought was just a crazy tale, than handed the man a drink and said:

"You may drink this at my expense, on condition that you don't repeat that cussed yarn any more in this place. Two or three tellin's of it would drive away the last customer forever."

And yet travelers to the Mammoth Cave confirm the traveling man's story.[91]

The Guides

Mammoth Cave is a confusing maze of winding passages that may loop around to bring you back where you started or get you hopelessly lost. There are no stars or sun for guidance. Pits, canyons, and jagged rocks abound. There are no plants to eat and water can be hard to find. It is not a place you want to be if you do not know where you're going or what you're doing, so ever since tours began in 1816, there have been cave guides to lead visitors safely through.

When tours took the place of saltpeter mining at the cave in 1816, some of the mining operation managers and their sons became the first cave guides. Cave owner Fleming Gatewood sold his share of Mammoth Cave while it was being mined, but he and his family continued to work at the cave after tourism began. Fleming's son, George Slaughter Gatewood, left his mark on the cave as a guide. George Gatewood did not have much historic impact; however, he literally left his mark all over the cave walls and ceiling. Modern cave visitors can still see his name and initials written with the soot of smoky candles in many places in the cave.

Other than knowing of them—Gatewood, Archibald Miller, and Schackleford—little is known about the lives of these miners-turned-guides.

A new type of guide appeared at the cave in 1837, when Franklin Gorin from Glasgow, Kentucky, bought Mammoth Cave and the hotel. Gorin brought with him a young slave named Stephen Bishop. The miner-guides taught Stephen[*] the art of cave guiding. Soon, Stephen and other slaves replaced paid guides at the cave.

Stephen not only learned the established tour routes but probed

---

[*] I refer to Stephen Bishop by his first name because historical accounts refer to him as Stephen.

The only known drawing of Stephen Bishop was published after his death. Did the artist meet Stephen years earlier, or did he base the drawing on descriptions? This 21st century artwork by Bonnie Curnock is based on the 19th century drawing.

farther into the cave to discover previously unknown passages that became new tour routes. Stephen's skill as a guide and an explorer made him a celebrity at Mammoth Cave. The famous author Baryard Taylor toured the cave with Stephen and wrote about him in his book, *At Home and Abroad* in 1855:

> Stephen, who has had a share in all the principal explorations and discoveries, is almost as widely known as the Cave itself. ... I think no one can travel under his guidance without being interested in the man, and associating him in memory with the realm over which he is chief ruler.[92]

Stephen's fame extended overseas. The book *An Englishwoman's Experience in America* called him "the prince of guides ... he seems more like the high-priest and expounder of its mysteries, than a hired guide, much less a slave."[93]

Stephen even accompanied people in their dreams. One account claims that the hotel landlord said "some of his guests had made a terrible noise in the night, and called out lustily for Stephen, the guide!"[94]

Perhaps the most impressive description of Stephen Bishop was from his master, Franklin Gorin, who spoke of Stephen more as a respected colleague than as a slave.

> I placed a guide in the Cave—the celebrated and great STEPHEN. ... Stephen was a self-educated man; he had a fine genius, a great fund of wit and humor, some little knowledge of Latin and Greek, and much knowledge of geology; but his great talent was a perfect knowledge of man.
>
> ... I owned Stephen's mother and brother, but not until after both of the children were born. Stephen was certainly a very extraordinary boy and man. His talents were of the first order. He was trustworthy and reliable; he was companionable: he was a hero, and could be a clown. He knew a gentleman or a lady as if by instinct. He learned whatever he wished, without trouble or labor, and it is said that a late professor of geology spoke highly of his knowledge in that department of science.[95]

Unlike many slaves, Stephen Bishop could write. He left his signature throughout Mammoth Cave. Photo by Rick Olson.

*The Old Guide's Cemetery is named for Stephen Bishop,
the only guide buried there.*

Gorin sold Mammoth Cave and Stephen to Dr. John Croghan in 1839. Dr. Croghan apparently also thought highly of Stephen. The doctor had Stephen draw a map of the cave for the book *Rambles in the Mammoth Cave*, published in 1845. "By Stephen Bishop, One of the Guides" is printed in large letters on the map. The map is not very accurate compared to modern surveys of the cave, but considering that Stephen drew the map from memory without the aid of survey equipment, it is impressive. Dr. Richard Ellworth Call, co-author of *The Mammoth Cave of Kentucky, An Illustrated Manual*, published in 1902, felt that Stephen's map was the best map of the cave.[96]

Shortly before Dr. Croghan died in 1849, he wrote in his will that all his slaves would be freed seven years after his death. He instructed his trustees to hire out the slaves for wages "as to prepare them for freedom and to provide the means for their support and removal to Liberia or elsewhere. ..."[97] The Jefferson County Court Order and Minute Book states that Stephen Bishop, his wife Charlotte, their 13-year-old son Thomas, and Croghan's other slaves gained their freedom on February 4, 1856.[98] Stephen apparently had no plans to move to Liberia or anywhere else because eight months later he bought 75 acres near Mammoth Cave.[99]

Stephen did not have long to enjoy his freedom or his land. He died of unknown causes in 1857, at about 37 years old (his exact birth date is unknown). Modern cave guides, cave explorers, and other fans of Stephen Bishop have pondered the cause of his death—

was he sick, did he have a tragic caving accident, was he murdered? A letter written by the famous astronomer Maria Mitchell who toured Mammoth Cave in May 1857 makes sickness look likely (see page 68 for more on Maria Mitchell). She wrote, "I called the landlord as soon as we arrived at the Cave House, and asked if we could have Mat, who I had been told was the best guide now that Stephen is ill."[100] Stephen passed away soon after Mitchell's visit and was buried in an unmarked grave.

Several years after Stephen's death, James R. Mellon visited Mammoth Cave. Like many other travelers who had read about the cave and Stephen, Mellon hoped the famous guide would take him in the cave. Upon learning that Stephen was dead and had no tombstone, Mellon promised Stephen's widow, Charlotte, that he would send a marker for the grave. He bought a tombstone originally made for a Civil War Union soldier whose family could not pay for it. The soldier's name was removed and replaced with Stephen Bishop's name[101] and incorrect year of his death—1859. Assuming the marker was put in the right place, Stephen is buried in the Old Guide's Cemetery, named for him, near the modern Mammoth Cave Hotel.

Stephen still holds high status at Mammoth Cave; he is a hero and a role model to modern cave guides, explorers, and visitors. Once, a self-proclaimed psychic came to Mammoth Cave and said Stephen had told her he was displeased with modern cave guides because they were mistaken about the date of his death. Another psychic claimed Stephen was pleased with the guides for holding him in high regard. Mammoth Cave guides like to believe the second psychic was right.

Two other young slaves, Nicholas Bransford and Materson Bransford, were brought to Mammoth Cave to work as guides about the same time as Stephen. Nick and Mat Bransford were probably not related—their shared last name was that of their master, Thomas Bransford. Thomas was Mat's father, but their relationship was master and slave rather than father and son. The cave's owners Franklin Gorin, John Croghan, and Croghan's heirs leased Nick and Mat from Thomas Bransford Sr. and eventually from his son (Mat's half-brother), Thomas L. Bransford.

As slaves, the guides were not paid wages, but they found ways to earn money. Asa Walker, a Civil War soldier, wrote in his journal that he paid Nick a dollar to catch some eyeless fish for him.[102] F.J. Stevenson, another Civil War era traveler, wrote that Nick had used

Cave guides Mat and Nick Bransford at the Historic Entrance in 1866.
Photograph by Charles Waldack.

the money he earned catching cave fish to buy his freedom "some years" before Stevenson's 1863 visit. He described fishing in the cave with Nick:

> Nick kicked up the sand on the river bank and produced a small hand-net, which he had buried there by way of hiding it from the other nigger, and we waded into the stream up to our knees, he going first with the net and I following with the basket of provision, etc. He waded very cautiously on so as not to disturb the water, and presently I saw something white darting from side to side and bumping itself against the rocks in a foolish wild way that was very curious. By-and-by it settled perfectly motionless in the water as if stunned, and being well within reach of Nick's net, he very gently and slowly lowered it into the water just in front of the fish's nose, and the next moment the creature was corked up safely in a bottle that Nick had brought with him for the purpose.[103]

Mat Bransford was still a slave in 1863,† but an article in the

---

† The Emancipation Proclamation issued by Lincoln in 1863 declared slaves in the Confederate states free, but did not apply to slaves in the border state of Kentucky, which was still part of the Union.

*Mat Bransford with the tools of his trade – a lunch basket,
a fuel can and the indispensable lantern.*

August 20, 1863, edition of the *Louisville Daily Journal* makes it appear he had some degree of freedom and respect that few slaves had. He apparently was able to visit Louisville not as a slave attending his owner's needs, but for his own pleasure.

No one that has visited Mammoth Cave during the last quarter of a century has forgotten Mat, the colored guide, to whose attentions they have been indebted for most of their pleasurable remembrances of a visit to that great subterranean wonder. ... He is a native of Nashville, Tenn., and is owned by Thom. L. Bransford, late of Nashville, but at present a seeker after "his rights" in the South. ... Although by no means scientific, he is familiar with the geographical

Nick Bransford, by Danish artist Joachim Ferdinand Richardt in 1857.

and chemical formations peculiar to the Cave, and discourses of all its wonders with an apparent knowledge of his subjects that would

A visitor's tribute to Nick Bransford in the Snowball Room in Mammoth Cave

do credit to Prof. Silliman.† Mat arrived in this city yesterday, and is a guest of our friends at the Louisville Hotel.

He will sit for his portrait to-day at Brown's daguerrean saloon, after which he will take a shy at whatever is worth looking at above ground hereabout, returning to the Cave tomorrow.[104]

Even though Mat and the other slaves who guided at the cave had higher social status than most slaves, they still had to deal with the harsh realities of slavery. Mat's wife, Parthena, and their three children were owned by a farmer who lived near Mammoth Cave. Parthena's master sold the children away from them. Slave owners believed selling slave children to be like selling calves, not breaking up families. Even some abolitionists did not recognize black people as being emotionally and intellectually equal to whites. F. Rusling, an abolitionist, said to Mat, "I don't suppose you missed these children much? You colored people never do, they say."[105]

Mat Bransford and Stephen Bishop influenced abolitionist author Mattie Griffith, who wrote about a visit to Mammoth Cave in her 1859 novel, *Madge Vertner*. In the book, Mammoth Cave's owner is a fictional character, but Stephen and Matt (Griffith's spelling) are mentioned by name. Seeing that the guides, though slaves, had some authority and respect in the cave, Griffith wrote:

> The most aristocratic ladies and gentleman who visit the Cave seem to forget for a time those unnatural distinctions of race and caste, and associate with the colored guides in the most familiar manner. ... Truly, the Mammoth Cave should be the temple of abolitionism.[106]

Foreign visitors from countries where there was no slavery often commented on this peculiar institution they encountered in the American south. An Italian traveler who toured the cave in 1859 called slavery "a bad gangrene corroding the State of Kentucky."[107] An English visitor wrote about a conversation he had in the Mammoth Cave Hotel during the Civil War:

> As we sat by the fire in the evening, the little party consisting, in

---

† Benjamin Silliman was a well-known biologist from Yale who counted millions of bats at Mammoth Cave in the 1800s.

addition to us three Englishmen, of some of the people belonging to the hotel, and one or two neighboring Kentuckians, the conversation turned upon the agitated question of emancipation. The feeling in its favour which I found to prevail in the capital of the State, where some of the leading journals have become its strenuous supporters, did not appear to have penetrated as yet into the remoter part of the State. Some of the company talked just as you occasionally hear persons talk in England—"The condition of the slave is a happy one—he has no cares—he is clothed and fed, and that is all that he minds about, and when he is past work he is taken care of by his master."

"Who," said a hulking fellow, who seemed to me to have an uncommonly easy time of it, "Who will take care of me when I get too old to work?" ... My young countrymen seemed to have learned reticence to a painful extent for Englishmen, and when, in the course of the conversation, I felt constrained to say in a few words that I did not share in the opinions of the others about slavery, one of them came to me aside, with a kindly-meant caution, that it was not safe to say always what one thought in this country.[108]

With the end of the Civil War came freedom for the cave guides and hotel workers who had not been able to purchase their freedom or been emancipated by Dr. Croghan. After the Civil War, the guide force was made up of both black and white guides, who apparently worked together as equals. Mat Bransford's son Henry, his grandson Matt, and other descendents continued the Bransford family tradition of cave guiding until the 1930s—nearly one hundred years of service to Mammoth Cave. The tradition was reborn in 2004, when Mat Bransford's great, great, grandson, Jerry Bransford, became a Mammoth Cave guide.

Famous Visitors

Because of Mammoth Cave's world-wide fame and status as a must-see destination for anyone touring the United States, the cave attracted many famous writers, artists, entertainers, dignitaries, and scientists from around the world.

Authors helped publicize Mammoth Cave by writing about their underground adventures. Robert Montgomery Bird—a medical doctor turned poet, playwright, novelist, and artist—wrote one of the first books on the cave, *Peter Pilgrim: or, A Rambler's Recollections* in 1838. Who would not want to visit Mammoth Cave after reading Bird's testimonial?

> I recommend all broken-hearted lovers and dyspeptic dandies to carry their complaints to the Mammoth Cave, where they will undoubtedly find themselves "translated" into very buxom and happy persons, before they are aware of it.[109]

Bird's other well-known works include the play *The Gladiator* and the novel *Nick of the Woods*. A man of many talents, Bird also did paintings of the Mammoth Cave entrance and some buildings that he called The old Cabin (Gatewood's house) at the Mammoth Cave. In the 1840s and 1850s, he experimented with the new art of photography, which he called "sun-painting,"[110] though he did not take any photos at Mammoth Cave.

Author Bayard Taylor combined his passions for writing and traveling by writing many popular travel logs in the mid 1800s. Taylor and some friends traipsed across Europe for two years living on six cents a day. Taylor collected the letters he had written to newspapers about their adventures and misadventures into the popular book *View A-foot, or, Europe Seen with a Knapsack and Staff*, published in 1846.

Taylor wrote books about his travels in California, Colorado, Sweden, Denmark, and Lapland. He also wrote fiction and poetry, including the novel *Hannah Thurston: a Story of American life*.[111] Taylor wrote about his visit to Mammoth Cave in his 1855 book *At Home and Abroad*. Mammoth Cave was closer to home than many of the locales he wrote about, but his description makes it sound other-worldly:

> For in the cave you forget that there is an outer world somewhere above you. The hours have no meaning: time ceases to be: no thought of labor, no sense of responsibility, no twinge of conscience, intrudes to suggest the existence you have left. You walk in some limbo beyond the confines of actual life, yet no nearer the world of spirits. For my part I could not shake off the impression that I was wandering on the outside of Uranus or Neptune, or some planet still more deeply buried in the frontier darkness of our solar system.[112]

Magazine writer and editor Nathaniel Parker Willis did his part to make Mammoth Cave sound colorful and spectacular in his 1853 book *Health Trip to the Tropics*. He wrote, "Why, the state apartments of Versailles are not half so sumptuously ornamented as this portion of the basement story of Kentucky."[113] In the 1840s, Willis started and edited the magazine the *National Press*, which is still published today as *Town & Country*. [114] *

The famous writer and lecturer Ralph Waldo Emerson was visiting Cincinnati in 1850 when some friends convinced him to make a spur-of-the-moment trip to Mammoth Cave. The unplanned jaunt to the cave made a lasting impression on Emerson. He included his Mammoth Cave experience in his essay *Illusions*, published in 1860, about life's many illusions.

> Some years ago, in company with an agreeable party, I spent a long summer day in exploring the Mammoth Cave in Kentucky.
> ... But I then took notice and still chiefly remember that the best thing which the cave had to offer was an illusion. On arriving at what is called the "Star-Chamber," our lamps were taken from us by the guide and extinguished or put aside, and, on looking

---

* To find more of Bird's, Taylor's, and Willis' quotes on Mammoth Cave sprinkled throughout the book, see the endnotes.

The gypsum "stars" on the ceiling made Star Chamber popular with many cave visitors, including Ralph Waldo Emerson.

upwards, I saw or seemed to see the night heaven thick with stars glimmering more or less brightly over our heads, and even what seemed a comet flaming among them. ... I sat down on the rocky floor to enjoy the serene picture. Some crystal specks in the black ceiling high overhead, reflecting the light of a half-hid lamp, yielded this magnificent effect.

I own I did not like the cave so well for eking out its sublimities with his theatrical trick. But I have had many experiences like it, before and since; and we must be content to be pleased without too curiously analyzing the occasions.[115]

Emerson also described his cave trip in a letter to his wife, Lidian.

> We had also bought at Louisville the last bundle of Roman
> Candles in the city. ... When we came to great enlargements we
> lit a Roman Candle & discharged its dazzling fireballs into some
> yawning vault. No height or depth could resist their prying eyes.[116]

The letter mentioned that Stephen Bishop was his guide, but in spite of Emerson's strong abolitionist views, he did not comment on

*This 1871 drawing of the Historic Entrance is titled The Mouth
of the Cave. You can see why Melville compared it to the
mouth of the whale in Moby Dick.*

the guides' slavery. Emerson wrote essays to express his opinion, but the letter was to describe a fun adventure in Mammoth Cave to his wife, rather than to make a point.

Both Herman Melville and Jules Verne helped publicize Mammoth Cave in their writing. Melville or Verne may have visited Mammoth Cave without fanfare; in spite of their fame, few people would have recognized their faces. Or the writers may have only known the cave through its reputation; there is no record of either of them visiting the cave.

In his famous novel Moby Dick, published in 1851, Herman Melville compared the great whale, Moby Dick, to the great cave. He wrote:

> Let us now with whatever levers and steam-engines we have at hand, cant over the sperm whale's head, so that it may lie bottom up; then, ascending by a ladder to the summit, have a peep down the mouth; and were it not that the body is now completely separated from it, with a lantern we might descend into the great Kentucky Mammoth Cave of his stomach.[117]

In *A Journey to the Center of the Earth*, (1864) Jules Verne's characters descend into the interior of the earth, an endless cave that is a world in itself. Harry, the main character, compares the center of the earth to caves.

> I had read of most wonderful and gigantic caverns—but none in any way like this.
>
> The great grotto of Guachara, in Columbia, visited by the learned Humboldt; the vast and partially explored Mammoth Cave in Kentucky; what were these holes in the earth to that in which I stood in speechless admiration![118]

The nineteenth century conservationist, writer, and Sierra Club founder John Muir is best known for his work to protect the natural wonders of the west, especially Yosemite National Park, but he also appreciated and wrote about the natural beauty of the eastern states. In 1867, he journeyed on foot from Indianapolis, Indiana, to Cedar Key, Florida, and recorded his adventure in his book, *A Thousand-Mile Walk to the Gulf*. Mammoth Cave was among his stops. Before arriving at the cave, Muir talked to a local man at the nearby town of Horse Cave.

He told me that he had never been at Mammoth Cave—that it was not worth going 10 miles to see, as it was nothing but a hole in the ground, and I found that his was no rare case. He was one of the useful, practical men—too wise to waste precious time with weeds, caves, fossils, or anything else that he could not eat.

Arrived at the great Mammoth Cave, I was surprised to find it in so complete naturalness. A large hotel with fine walks and gardens is near it. But fortunately the cave has been unimproved, and were it not for the narrow trail that leads down the glen to its door, one would not know that it had been visited. ...

I never before saw Nature's grandeur in so abrupt contrast with paltry artificial gardens. The fashionable hotel grounds are in exact parlor taste, with many a beautiful plant cultivated to deformity, and arranged in strict geometrical beds, the whole pretty affair a laborious failure side by side with Divine beauty.[119]

Photography was a new art in the 1800s and a dark cave was a difficult subject to photograph in the days before electric lights, but several well-known artists captured Mammoth Cave's grandeur on canvas. Paintings gave people who had not been to the cave a glimpse of it, sparking their curiosity.

The artist, Regis Francois Gignoux, painted *Interior of Mammoth Cave* in 1843. The young French artist moved from France to the United States in 1840 and became famous for his paintings of nature. Gignoux's work was so high in demand that art collectors commissioned paintings faster than he could paint them. His most famous painting, *Niagara Falls in Winter*, hangs in the Senate wing of the United States Capitol.[120] Most of Gignoux's paintings of natural scenes are considered more realistic than those of many American artists in the mid-1800s, but he used some artistic license with *Interior of Mammoth Cave*. The painting, showing the Historic Entrance from the inside looking out, makes the truly grand entrance passage look even bigger and more spectacular than it is. The New York Historical Society restored *Interior of Mammoth Cave* for its Henry Luce III Center for the Study of American Culture.

Danish landscape artist Joachim Ferdinand Richardt was also attracted to the magnificent landscapes of the United States. He painted many famous natural wonders, including New Hampshire's White Mountains, Virginia's Natural Bridge, and the waterfalls of Yosemite. Like Gignoux and many other nineteenth century artists,

The Mammoth Cave Hotel was one of many subjects the well known Danish artist Joachim Ferdinand Richardt drew while visiting the cave in the spring of 1857.

Niagara Falls was among Richardt's favorite subjects. His pursuit of scenes to paint brought Richardt to Mammoth Cave for a week in the spring 1857. Richardt made about 20 drawings at the cave. Along with the cave, he drew the Mammoth Cave Hotel and portraits of his cave guides, Mat and Nick Bransford. After leaving the cave, Richardt used sketches of the cave to paint six paintings in 1858 and 1859. The

This watercolor of the hotel was painted by a visitor named Mrs. P.R. Beall in 1893. Notice the differences in the building between this painting and Richardt's drawing done 37 years earlier. Some of the changes may be additions, wear, or repairs to the hotel; some may be artistic license.

This and the following sketches by Joachim Ferdinand Richardt are among several he made below and above ground while visiting the cave in 1857. The Bridal Altar in Gothic Avenue was popular with many artists and photographers.

Bottomless Pit.

location of four of Richardt's Mammoth Cave paintings is a mystery; they may belong to private collectors. They are titled, *Entrance to the Mammoth Cave, Entrance to the Mammoth Cave as Seen from the Inside, Washington Hall in Mammoth Cave,* and *Gothic Temple in Mammoth Cave.* As of 2006, two of Richardt's Mammoth Cave paintings, *Echo River in the Mammoth Cave, 1859* and *Echo River, 1857* belong to the Charleston Renaissance Gallery in Charleston, South Carolina.

Albert Tissandier was a French artist and journalist who was famous not only for painting and writing, but for balloon travel experiments he did with his brother, Gaston. In 1883, the brothers

In Richardt's sketch of an underground river, the guides are wading instead of boating. Are they going to retrieve a boat that drifted away from the bank?

designed "La France," the first electric powered airship.[123]

Recording his travels with his pen and paintbrush, Albert Tissandier toured America in 1885 and 1886. He visited Mammoth Cave in May 1885. In addition to a regular cave tour, Tissandier wanted extra time in order to sketch. The manager of the cave, Henry Ganter, knew Tissandier's art would bring publicity, so he was happy to provide him with a private guide, Henry Bransford. In his book, *Six Months in the United States*, Tissandier wrote:

> When I explained that my objective was to make sketches in order to preserve the memory of the marvels of the caverns, all difficulties were smoothed away and I was able to spend seven hours in Mammoth Cave.

He used his sketches to make nine drawings of sites in Mammoth Cave, including the Historic Entrance, the Grand Gallery, and Gothic Chapel. Tissandier's Mammoth Cave drawings now belong to the Utah Museum of Fine Arts.

Clement Reeves Edwards owned a photography and portrait painting studio in Bowling Green, Kentucky. Along with portraits, he painted landscapes, including *Mammoth Cave in 1859*. He may have visited Mammoth Cave several times, since he lived only about 40 miles away. Reeves also used a painting of the cave's Historic Entrance as a backdrop for portraits he took of people. These photos were often made into cartes-de-vistas, or visiting cards, with "Ready for Mammoth Cave" printed on them.[125] Cartes-de-vistas, often showing famous people, were popular for collecting and trading in the mid to late nineteenth century, similar to baseball cards.

Edwards was not as famous as Gignoux, Richardt, or Tissandier, but locally he was well-known and respected. In 2005, Edwards' work (and Mammoth Cave) was introduced to an audience far from Kentucky. His painting, *Mammoth Cave in 1859*, was sent to the U. S. Embassy in Riga, Latvia, for temporary display.

Mammoth Cave was popular with musicians and singers; listening to musical instruments and voices echo in the cave, especially on underground rivers, was always a hit. Most musicians who played in the cave were amateurs or small-time professionals, but two of the nineteenth century's most famous musical performers visited Mammoth Cave.

Norwegian violinist Ole Bull toured the cave in 1845. He was more popular with common folk than with European music critics, but he had many fans in the United States. Bull made five American concert tours, impressing people with Norwegian folk music and songs he wrote with American titles like, *Niagara* and *To the Memory of Washington*.[127]

An article from the June 26, 1845, edition of the *Salem Register*, from Salem, Massachusetts, mentioned Bull's Mammoth Cave visit.

Ole Bull took his violin into the cave and gave us some of his noblest performances, at the points most remarkable for their wonderful echoes. The music was like no earthly music. It seemed, indeed, superhuman. The whole company were as mute and motionless as statues, and tears, copious and gushing tears, streamed from every eye.[128]

The cave chamber he played in is still called Ole Bull's Concert Hall.

The Swedish singer Jenny Lind arrived at Mammoth Cave with more fanfare than any other 1800s celebrity. Known as "the Swedish Nightingale," she was the nineteenth century's female version of Elvis (ok, some similarities, some differences). Even in the days before radio, television, and sound recordings, Jenny Lind's fame spread across the western world. A locomotive, clipper ships,

The nineteenth century's most famous singer, Jenny Lind, created quite a stir when she visited Mammoth Cave.

songs, dances, a soup, and a town were named after her. Even today, cribs with spiral posts are called Jenny Lind cribs.

P.T. Barnum, the famous showman and founder of Barnum and Bailey's Circus, managed Lind's American concert tour in 1850 through 1852. Charles U. Shreve's description of Lind's concert in Louisville is a sample of the hub-bub she caused.

> For both concert nights Mozart Hall was packed almost to suffocation. ... Some hundreds were jammed in the corridor and on the stairs. ... Several thousand people were crowded up and down Jefferson and Fourth streets and on the surrounding buildings. So great was the power of Jenny Lind's voice that they could hear her almost as well as those within the hall. In my life before or since I never saw such enthusiasm as that aroused by her when she sang "Comin' Thro' the Rye." Men and women in

full dress sprang upon their seats and cheered themselves hoarse. They waved their hats and handkerchiefs. The stage was literally showered with flowers.[129]

Lind's concerts were in big cities that could attract large audiences, but no trip to America would be complete without a visit to Mammoth Cave, so she journeyed into rural Kentucky. She saw the trip to the cave as recreation, though other people at the cave hoped for more. Charles Shreve was also at the cave that day.

The next morning 300 or 400 people arrived at the cave from the surrounding country. They had heard of Jenny Lind's arrival and gathered there for the purpose of catching a glimpse of her and in the hope of hearing her sing, though there had been no arrangement for any performance at that place. It became known that Jenny Lind and her party were going through the cave that day and almost everyone there decided to go in also. Most of the crowd started before the concert company left the hotel and all of us stopped in the star chamber to wait for the great singer. ... it occurred to me that it would be an event of a lifetime if Jenny Lind could be prevailed upon to sing here in the star chamber. ... How her great voice, I thought, would fill the vaulted chambers with wondrous melody, and how its silvery tones would ring and reverberate through the distant caverns.

So we were determined to ask her and it was agreed that Billy Vertres ... should act as spokesman. Jenny Lind came into the star chamber leaning on the arm of her tenor, Belletti, who was said to be her sweetheart at that time. Barnum's representative, I am sorry to say, was not very far behind. At their approach Vertres put on his sweetest smile and stepping forward, addressed the singer in courtly terms. He said that nearly all of the people standing there in the cavern had come a long distance to see her and hear her sing.

* * * * * * * *

Jenny Lind smiled and seemed to be hesitating, while Barnum's agent drew nearer and looked unpleasant. Then the singer answered that her poor voice would sound but weak and out of place in such a wonderful cathedral make by the hand of God ... her engagements with Mr. Barnum were so exacting that she could not comply with the request. I'll tell you we felt flat and disappointed at this and were a good deal provoked at first, though she was, no doubt, right in living up to her agreement with Barnum.[130]

In the days before television and movies, actors were not as famous or recognizable as they are today, but the stage did have its stars. The Shakespearian actor Edwin Booth was one of the nineteenth century's greatest and most famous actors. Booth came from a theatrical family. His brother, John Wilkes Booth, and their father, Junius Brutus Booth, were also actors. Theatre historians are familiar with the Booth family's success on stage, but most people connect the Booth name with only one theatre—Ford's Theatre, where John Wilkes killed President Abraham Lincoln in 1865. John Wilkes's drop from actor to assassin set Edwin's acting career back temporarily, but he did return to the stage and went on to establish two theatres, the Booth Theatre, which no longer exists, and the Players' Club, which still stands in New York City.[131]

Edwin Booth visited Mammoth Cave in 1876. He wrote to his daughter about his cave tour and his guide, William Garvin.

> Our guide was a bright young colored chap, who produced by his imitations of dogs, cows, etc., some fine effects of ventriloquism on our way through the cave. In pointing out to us a huge stone shaped like a coffin he would remark: "Dis is de giant's coff-in," then, taking us to the other dilapidated side of it: "Dis is what he coughed out." . . . we went laughing at his weak jokes; for it was funny to us actors to see this fellow throwing his wit at us, and our appreciation of his acting made him very happy.[132]

A ledge in Mammoth Cave bears the name Booth's Amphitheatre. Legend has it, Booth climbed onto this rock and recited lines from Hamlet. In the late twentieth century, cave guides could push a button to play a recording of Hamlet's soliloquy, "To be or not to be: that is the question ..." in remembrance of Booth's underground performance. If Booth did perform in the cave, he did not mention it in his letter to his daughter.

Scientists were naturally attracted to Mammoth Cave. Sometime between 1818 and 1815, the naturalist Constantine Rafinesque visited Mammoth Cave for geological and zoological research, though he found Kentucky's caves "not the least interesting." He had little faith in the maps and information available on Mammoth Cave; he wrote:

> I also made a correct map of it as far as I went, which is very different from those popular catch-penny maps already published. In fact, all the popular accounts of this cave, inserted in the ephemeral press, are quite false, exaggerated, or fabulous.[133]

In the 1800s, many people assumed the cave extended under Green River. Rafinesque noticed the cave appeared to have been formed by underground rivers that flowed into Green River, causing him to doubt (correctly) that the cave could pass under the river.[134]

Rafinesque was almost as famous for his odd appearance and behavior as he was for his scientific genus. It is not surprising that he was drawn to Mammoth Cave, with its strange cave creatures that are so different from the familiar animals of the surface world. He was always searching for new species unknown to science. His friend John Jay Audubon, famous for his studies and paintings of birds, took advantage of Rafinesque's interest in undiscovered species with a little joke. Audubon gave Rafinesque sketches and descriptions of several new fish, including a 10-foot, 400 pounder called the devil-Jack diamond-fish. Unbeknownst to Rafinesque, the newly discovered fish existed only in Audubon's imagination. The joke backfired when Rafinesque gave Audubon credit for discovering the non-existent fish in his book *Ichthyologiea Ohiensis: Natural History of the Fishes Inhabiting the River Ohio and Its Tributary Streams*, published in 1820.[134]

Rafinesque's work at the cave earned him the honor of having a passage, Rafinesques Hall, in Mammoth Cave named after him. He also has his own bat—Rafinesque's big eared bat—which can be seen in trees and old buildings around Mammoth Cave National Park. Audubon never made it to the cave, but the passage Audubon Avenue was named for the Kentucky native.

Astronomer Maria Mitchell, one of the few women to achieve notoriety as a scientist in the 1800s, toured Mammoth Cave in 1857. Mitchell discovered a comet that became known as "Miss Mitchell's Comet." She was the first woman to become a member of the American Academy of Arts and Sciences, the Association for the Advancement of Science, and the American Philosophical Society. Mitchell helped establish the American Association for the Advancement of Women, and was a professor of astronomy at Vassar College in New York.[136]

Mitchell and a friend visited the cave for fun rather than scientific research. In spite of her achievements in what at the time was considered a man's world, she wrote in her journal:

> I was a little doubtful about the propriety of going to the Mammoth Cave without a gentleman escort, but if two ladies travel alone they must have the courage of men.[137]

Scientists have shown an interest in caves for a long time, but darkness, pits, and other obstacles kept early scientists (and almost everyone else) from going far underground. Edouard Martel, a French lawyer and caver, encouraged scientists and explorers to go underground by leading European cave expeditions beginning in 1888. Many cavers regard Martel as the father of speleology— the science of caves. In 1912, Martel came to Mammoth Cave. He expressed disappointment during his visit—not with the cave, but with the lack of one of his favorite caving supplies—alcohol:

E.A. Martel, the father of modern speleology.

> I felt most irritated by the strict application of the anti-alcohol laws in the dry State of Kentucky. Two long days spent in a damp, dark giant catacomb, with nothing to drink other than aqua simplex ("pure water" would be a misnomer), herb tea, or ginger

beer (which tastes like sugared pepper). And the same thing above in the hotel: Water, tea, or ginger beer to accompany extremely poor meals. A horror to European speleologists! Without a small bottle of rum from my personal luggage I could never have finished this very strenuous visit to Hovey's Cathedrals.[138]

Martel saw rum, wine, or brandy as indispensable when caving, but modern cavers recommend that you wait until you are safely out of the cave to partake.

Martha Washington never slept here, but guide William Garvin thought he saw her "ghost" in Mammoth Cave. Martha's ghost is conjured up with lantern (or today, electric) light.

Mammoth Cave's world-wide fame also attracted political leaders. Brazil's Emperor Dom Pedro II visited the cave in the mid 1800s. Dom Pedro, the grandson of the King of Portugal, became emperor of Brazil in 1831 at the tender age of five, when his father, Emperor Pedro I, abdicated the throne and returned to Portugal.[139]

Cave City resident S.J. Preston had the honor of escorting Emperor Dom Pedro and his party from Cave City to the cave by stagecoach. An old story says that at a rest stop everyone in the group except Mr. Preston removed their hats while Dom Pedro drank. A member of the party told Preston that it was proper to remove one's hat while with a sovereign. Preston answered, "I am a Kentuckian and somewhat of a sovereign myself." The emperor was said to have been so impressed by Preston's pluck that he offered him a sugar plantation if he returned to Brazil with him.[140] Preston did not take him up on the offer.

The Grand Duke Alexis of Russia was another noble to visit Mammoth Cave. He was greeted at the cave (and across America) with much fanfare in 1872. The son of Russia's Czar Alexander II, the Grand Duke was on a goodwill tour of the United States and Canada. The Grand Duke's popularity was due partially to Russia's support for the Union during the Civil War, but his dashing good looks and royal charm probably also helped him win admirers.

To break up the monotony of formal dinners and political speeches, the adventurous young Duke was sent on a buffalo hunt in Nebraska. There he met Lieutenant Colonel George Armstrong Custer, who continued to accompany the Duke in his travels across America, including a four-hour tour of Mammoth Cave. "The Duke at the Cave," an article from the Louisville *Courier-Journal* in February, 1872, stated a special train was arranged to take the Duke, Custer, and his party to the cave.[141] Another Louisville *Courier-Journal* article, "Royalty Underground, The Grand Duke Alexis Ten Miles in Mammoth Cave," said the Duke's party enjoyed watching a flaming piece of paper drop into Bottomless Pit, hearing about Indian mummies, and seeing the saltpeter mining ruins.[142]

Newspaper articles focused on the Duke's visit to the cave with only a brief mention of Custer being part of the party. Today, Americans are more familiar with George Armstrong Custer than the Grand Duke Alexis. Custer's most famous battle, Little Big Horn, had not yet occurred when the Duke and Custer visited Mammoth Cave [obviously]. Custer may have been seen as just another military officer, while the foreign, royal Duke may have been viewed as a more romantic and exciting person to meet.

Two kings whom newspapers claimed visited Mammoth Cave may never have made it. According to a December 9, 1916, article from the *Louisville Times*, England's King Edward's name was signed in the Mammoth Cave Hotel register, which had been destroyed in a fire that morning. An article in the Louisville *Courier Journal* in 1936 stated Edward's son, King George, had signed the hotel register.[143] Some of the registers supposedly lost in the fire have been found and are now at the Kentucky Library at Western Kentucky University, but none of them have the signatures of either British king.

One of the surviving hotel registers from 1863 does have "Abraham Lincoln, President of the U. States" written in it. Alas, it is unlikely that Lincoln (a Kentucky native) ever graced Mammoth Cave. The handwriting does not match authentic Lincoln signatures.[144] While many famous people could have visited Mammoth Cave anonymously if they wished, the president's face was well known, and he would have arrived with an entourage, so it is unlikely he would have been unnoticed.

For Your Health

Nineteenth century tourists were drawn to Mammoth Cave primarily for the same reason modern cave visitors are—to enjoy exploring the cave. But some people believed a trip into the cave was also good for your health.

The belief that the cave had healing powers goes back to the saltpeter mining days before and during the War of 1812. Author Robert Montgomery Bird visited the cave in the 1830s when former saltpeter managers were guiding cave tours. He heard stories about the wonderful health of the slaves and oxen that mined the saltpeter and wrote about them in his 1838 book *Peter Pilgrim: or A Rambler's Recollections*:

> The nitre-diggers were a famously healthy set of men: it was common and humane practice to employ labourers of enfeeble constitutions, who were soon restored to health and strength, though kept at constant labour: and more joyous, merry fellows were never seen. The oxen, of which several were kept, day and night, in the cave hauling the nitrous earth, were, after a month or two of toil, in as fine condition for the shambles as if fattened in the stall.[145]

Ebenezer Meriam, who visited the cave in 1813 while mining was going on, claimed, "During the whole time this cave was wrought in for saltpetre, there was no case of sickness among the numerous workmen. They all enjoyed excellent and uninterrupted health."[146]

In spite of Meriam's claim, at least one saltpeter miner did get sick. Cave manager Archibald Miller wrote a letter to John Hendrick, the owner of a slave named Tambo who was leased to mine saltpeter at Mammoth Cave.

Mammoth Cave Jany 13th Jany 1814
Mr. John Hendrick
Dear Sir; your Boy Tambo is very sick and I wish you to come over and see him I was expecting you on Sunday (crossed out) munday Last. I have bled him Twice and will give him A swett to day I have got no medican at present. I wish you to come and see him and come as soon as you can. [*sic*]
Respectfully

A. Miller[147]

A person did not have to work in Mammoth Cave all day, every day to benefit from the cave's healing powers. Visitors on tours lasting a few hours wrote about how good they felt. The pure cave air and water were reputed to help lung disorders,[148] cure chronic dysentery and diarrhea,[149] and relieve colds.[150] The most common health benefit reported was extra energy. An article in the January, 1852 issue of *The International Magazine of Literature, Art, and Science* stated:

The amount of exertion which can be performed here without fatigue, is astonishing. The superabundance of oxygen in the atmosphere operates like moderate doses of exhilarating gas. The traveler feels a buoyant sensation, which tempts him to run and jump, and leap from crag to crag and bound over the stones in his path.[151]

A German visitor made a similar claim in 1870, "The remarkably clear air of all parts of the Cave is so bracing that even weak people, scarcely able to take a short walk outside, are only slightly tired by a walk of many hours in the Cave."[152]

The cave air was believed to be so pure and invigorating that when leaving the cave, the surface air seemed "insufferably offensive"[153] by comparison. Godfrey Vigne, a lawyer who visited the cave in 1831, recommended that travelers pause at the cave entrance when leaving to get use to the change in air. He warned, "Those who do not take the precaution of waiting a few minutes, are almost invariably attacked with giddiness, or a fainting fit."[154]

Ralph Seymour Thompson, author of the 1879 book *The Sucker's Visit to the Mammoth Cave*, recognized the healthy cave for what it really was—cool on a hot summer day.

Early visitors may have been tempted to run and leap in the cave, but it could be more dangerous than healthy, especially at cliffs like Lovers Leap.

Enthusiastic visitors to the Cave have written that a person feels no fatigue there, that miles are walked without weariness by persons who could not walk a half a mile at home. It is all nonsense. There is nothing in the cave to reverse the laws of nature, and flesh and blood are the same below ground as above.

The facts are that the air of the cave is cool, pure, and bracing,—and of course a person is capable of more exertion than he would be without this help. The many wonders of the cave, and the sense of strangeness, the constant attractions to the eye and ear, also remove the attention for the time being from the physical condition, and also act, undoubtedly, as a stimulus, enabling a person to draw heavily on the reserve power—just as a person will show unusual strength during a period of intense mental excitement.

But beyond this the cave has no power to prevent weariness.[155]

A doctor named John Croghan bought Mammoth Cave in 1839. His main interest in the cave was tourism, but he also wanted to take advantage of the reputed healthy atmosphere. In a letter written in 1839, Dr. Croghan mentioned the idea of establishing an underground resort that would be recreational and healthy.

> I remarked to one of the guides, Mr. Miller, you ought to have an Hotel, well supplied with refreshments of all kinds, chambers on one side for the ladies and the other for gentlemen, a handsomely furnished parlor, reading room and dining room, and all brilliantly illuminated. ... An Hotel under ground at the distance of 5 or 6 miles, and a stage to convey passengers thereto, is in itself so unique, that, I think uncommon with all whom I have heard speak as the subject, it would be a means of increasing greatly the number of visitors. ... Owing to the uniformity of temperature throughout the year 60 Fahrenheit, the dryness of the atmosphere, and the continual purification thereof by the constant formation of saltpetre, I have no doubt there is nowhere to be found a spot so desirable for persons laboring under pulmonary affections, chronic Rheumatism, diseases of the eye, etc. etc. Divesting myself of all selfish consideration I have no hesitation in affirming that for enjoyment, for gratification of ones curiosity—for the restoration & preservation of health it stands unrivaled and in fine is worth all the Niagaras and watering places in the Union put together.[156]

Dr. Croghan's underground hotel never came to be, but he had another plan. Dr. William McDowell, a physician from Louisville, believed that the cave's pure air would relieve the lung disease consumption (now commonly called tuberculosis) and asked about having a patient stay in the cave. The idea appealed to Dr. Croghan, so he set up an "invalids village" in the cave for tuberculosis patients, hoping they would be cured.

The 54-degree Fahrenheit temperature in the cave is cool and refreshing if you're hiking on a cave tour, but living every day in a cold cave with just limestone to look at would not be pleasant. Nevertheless, patients were willing to live in such uncomfortable and gloomy conditions because they hoped it would cure them. A traveler wrote in 1855 that some cedar trees had been planted near the patients' dining area, apparently to bring some color and cheer to the gray surroundings; but the trees, like people, are not meant to live in the dark.[157]

F.J. Stevenson, who visited the cave in 1863, 20 years after the tuberculosis experiment closed, looked at the huts that the patients had lived in. Stevenson and his guide, Nick Bransford, discussed how Dr. Croghan:

The huts that housed tuberculosis patients became tourist attractions after the experiment to cure tuberculosis in the cave failed in the 1840s.

... succeeded in persuading 13 wretched and deluded men, far gone with the disease, to make the experiment of trying to live there. ... Nick was in attendance on these consumptives during the four months they remained underground, and he pointed out a rock on which he used to stand and blow a horn to call the ghastly company to their meals. He said it was frightful to see them dropping in one by one like so many skeletons, and to hear their dreadful coughs as they came crawling along the avenues from the more distant cottages. Three of them died in there, and the rest took fright and went out immediately; but they all died a few weeks after their return to daylight. Nick was present at the deathbeds of those who died underground, and his description of the death struggles of one of them who died "kinder bad" (as he expressed it) was truly awful.[158]

In a letter dated January 12, 1843, one of the patients, O.H.P.

Anderson, wrote:

> I left the cave yesterday under an impression that I would be better out than in as my lungs were constantly irritated with smoke and my nose offended by a disagreeable effluvia, the necessary consequence of its being so tenanted without ventilation.
>
> ... I don't look as well as when I entered the cave. Others will leave the cave soon I think; two recently died. I am the 5th person who has left.
>
> Yours very truly,
> O.H.P. Anderson[159]

Dr. Croghan wrote a letter the next day:

> There are now from 15 to 20 invalids in the Cave. I am convinced they would all return to the land above with greatly improved healths, but for three considerations. 1st, the want of attention to diet, 2, their indiscriminate use of medicines and lastly, smoke. Whenever the temperature within the Cave corresponds with that without, smoke collects about the chambers, [and] by irritating the lungs, destroys measurably the good resulting from the uniformity of the Cave climate and the peculiarity of its air. By sinking a shaft in the vicinity of the "invalids village" (as Judge Tompkins styles it) this may be obviated.[160]

A chimney to get rid of the smoke was never made (Croghan would have had to bore through about 150 feet of limestone and sandstone). By the end of 1843, the patients gave up on the healing power of the cave and returned to the surface where they could spend their last days looking out a window at sunshine and color instead of gray limestone.

Dr. Croghan often complained about feeling poorly, coughing, and having trouble breathing. He died in 1849, possibly from tuberculosis.

Most of the huts that housed the tuberculosis patients were torn down in the 1800s, but two stone huts remain. Modern visitors stroll by the huts and peer in the doors and windows. The good news is the tuberculosis bacteria are dead; they do not survive long once they leave a living person. The bad news is the cave really has no healing powers, so other than temporary relief from pollen, you would not be cured of any illness.

"That Mysterious Race"

While touring Mammoth Cave in the 1830s, Harriet Martineau noticed cane reed torches left by ancient people who ventured into the cave thousands of years earlier. She pondered who left them there and wrote:

> It is supposed that this cave was made use of by that mysterious race which existed before the Indians, and of which so many curious traces remain in the middle States of the West: a race more civilized, to judge by the works of their hands, than the Indians have ever been; but of which no tradition remains.[161]

Martineau's belief that a mysterious race other than American Indians had left the torches and other artifacts in the cave was common in the 1800s. This "mysterious race" was also credited with building shell mounds, pyramids, and other impressive structures across North and South America. Many Americans of European decent believed that American Indians were incapable of such impressive work, but they were wrong. According to archaeologists, the artifacts in the cave were left by American Indians.

In spite of the common belief in a mysterious pre-Indian race, many early cave visitors realized American Indians had left the torches, gourds, slippers, and other artifacts scattered throughout the cave. Nineteenth century cave visitors had ideas about who these Indians were and what they did in Mammoth Cave, but it was not until the second half of the twentieth century that much was learned about them.

Prehistoric American Indians explored the cave mostly 2,000 to 2,800 years ago, but a few ventured into the cave as long ago as 4,100 years.[162] Curiosity, the same thing that drives modern people to explore caves, may have been part of what led American Indians into the dark passages. They were looking for more than adventure, though; the ancient cave explorers were in search of gypsum and other salts. Today, we use gypsum for drywall (and more importantly, Twinkies and beer) but we do not know what the American Indians at Mammoth Cave used gypsum for—maybe paint.[163] We know they mined gypsum because you can see where it has been battered off of the cave walls with stones and shells. They also gathered a salt called mirabilite from the cave to possibly use as a food preservative, a seasoning, or maybe even a laxative.[164]

Ancient American Indians stopped using Mammoth Cave about 2,000 years ago, though they continued to live above the cave. Maybe they no longer needed gypsum or mirabilite. When modern European Americans rediscovered the cave in the late 1700s, no American Indians were living in the area. The ancient cave explorers did not leave a written history, so we have only the tools, torches, and other artifacts that they left in the cave to learn about their story. Artifacts, though, are harder to read than written words.

Many early 1800s cave visitors reported seeing giant human bones, including a skeleton of a "giant 7 or 8 feet in height,"[165] a huge jaw, and a skull "of most astonishing thickness being at least double that of an ordinary skull."[166] Mammoth Cave was not the only site where giant bones were supposedly found; such reports were

An ancient American Indian caver left this slipper in the cave.
The knife is not an artifact, it is for scale. Photo by Rick Olson.

common across the country, causing many people to believe North America had once been inhabited by a giant race no longer living.

The supposed giant bones of the cave are long gone, so we do not know how big they were. The bones were probably ordinary size; early tourists often exaggerated. Also, it is easy for someone who does not know where arm and leg bones connect to the shoulders and hips to overestimate how tall a person was.

Mammoth and the surrounding caves not only had human bones, but mummies. These American Indian mummies were not like Egyptian mummies; they were not embalmed—the dry caves naturally dried and preserved the bodies.

Two mummies were found around 1814 in nearby Short Cave. Charles Wilkins, the owner of Mammoth Cave and Short Cave, wrote to the American Antiquarian Society about the mummies in 1817:

> I received information, that an infant, of nine or twelve months old, was discovered in a saltpetre Cave in Warren County, about four miles from the Mammoth Cave, in a perfect state of preservation. I hastened to the place; but, to my mortification, found that, upon its being exposed to the atmosphere, it had fallen into dust, and that its remains, except the skull, with all its clothing, had been thrown into the furnace. I regretted this much, and promised the labourers to reward them, if they would preserve the next subject for me. About a month afterwards, the present one was discovered, and information given to our agent at the Mammoth Cave, who sent immediately for it, and brought and placed it there, where it remained for twelve months.[167]

The adult mummy, a woman, eventually became known as Fawn Hoof because of a deer hoof necklace she wore. After being shown at Mammoth Cave, Fawn Hoof was taken to Lexington, New York, and other cities for display. The mummy became Mammoth Cave's first celebrity and helped to make the cave famous. One the cave's earliest tourists described Fawn Hoof and her finery in 1814:

> It is supposed to have been a Queen, from the number of trinkets found with it, consisting of needles, head dresses of various kinds of feathers, necklaces of deer hoofs, beads, mockasons, [sic]

paint, a whistle, a bear's jawbone, a hawk's claw, and a rattle-snake with rattles. These were enclosed in a pack, (or wallet, used by Indians for transporting goods), they being first enclosed in a fine wrought indispensable, afterwards in one of a coarser texture, and then in the pack; which with the body was wrapped up in two dressed deer skins, and the whole again enclosed in a mat or coarse wrapper. The visage seemed quite venerable, and the whole presented a truly antique appearance.[168]

Some early accounts describe Fawn Hoof as being as much as 6 feet tall, but an 1874 estimate put her height closer to 5 feet.[169] Like the giant bones, Fawn Hoof's size was exaggerated—if a 5-foot-tall mummy was good, a mummy bordering on giant size was better.

In 1914, Fawn Hoof and some of her belongings were taken to the Smithsonian Institution in Washington, D.C., where they remain today, though not on display.

In 1875, a mummy was found in the Salts Cave section of Mammoth Cave (Salts Cave was not known to be part of the Mammoth Cave system at the time). The cave explorers who found the mummy recorded their discovery with an inscription on a rock:

> Sir
> I have found one of the Grat wonders of the
> World in this cave, whitch is a muma
> Can all seed hereafter
> Found March the 8 1875
> T.E. lee J.L lee
> an W.d. Cutliff
> dicuvers [*sic*][170]

The mummy was believed to be a little girl and was called Little Alice. It was taken from Salts Cave and began a long career on display in Mammoth Cave, at the New Entrance (opened in 1921). The mummy has been at the Museum of Anthropology in Lexington, Kentucky, since 1970.

Not everyone approved of the mummy being removed from its resting place. There is a second inscription, known as "curse rock," near where Little Alice was found:

A slab of limestone called The Devils Looking Glass has ancient American Indian drawings as well as 1800s graffiti.

How are you grave robbers. What is it you would not do. They [*sic*] is nothing too mean for you to do. You low down scoundrels. What is it you wouldn't do. Just think for a sec of men to steal the dead ... [illegible, perhaps "just speculate on it"]. Sir you are worse than a murderer. Are you not afraid it will follow you in your paths of a day and your bed at night. You low down dirty thief of hell yours most ... [illegible, perhaps "respectfully"].

JM Smith

P.S. Call again you honest fellows when you get hard up for a few dimes or call at some other grave yard.

The writer, J.M. Smith, explored Salts Cave during the same time period as Little Alice's discoverers. His name is written with dates from the 1870s in several places in the cave.[171]

Archeologists studied Little Alice more closely in the twentieth century and found there had been some gender confusion; Little Alice was really Little Al. He was an American Indian boy about nine years old when he died in the cave about 2,000 years ago. He may have died from internal hemorrhage of the aorta, which could have been caused by a fall in the cave.[172]

Though many 1800s visitors enjoyed viewing American Indian

mummies as curiosities, J.M. Smith was not alone in thinking the remains should be treated with respect. W. Stump Forwood, the author of *An Historical and Descriptive Narrative of the Mammoth Cave of Kentucky*, toured Indian Cave, a local cave named for the American Indian bones found inside. When Forwood asked to see the bones, the guide told him the bones were not on display because they had:

> ... been sacrilegiously handled by some of the visitors, even to carrying them out and leaving them exposed upon the ground, he considered it his Christian duty to deposit them in a place where they would escape further desecration; he then pointed out to us a deep pit in the Cave, into the invisible depths of which he had thrown them.[173]

Cave Dogs, Cave Weddings, and Other Cave Adventures

Along with the routine tours and exploration, nineteenth century Mammoth Cave was the site of special events, unusual adventures, new technology, and interesting stories.

Often important characters in adventure tales, loyal canines abound in stories about discovering cave entrances but do not tend to venture far into caves. When visiting Mammoth Cave in 1838, Robert Montgomery Bird thought the cave guide's dog, Bull, might be smart for avoiding the cave.

> But first let us seduce honest Bull, the great dog that has been wagging his tail at us in token of friendship, to lead us to the cavern. "You may get him into the Hollow," quoth the guide, nodding his head; "but you won't get him into the cave; because dogs are exactly the people that won't go in, no way you can fix it.—They have a horror of it." Verily, after we had ourselves got in, and seen the last glimmer of fading daylight swallowed up in midnight gloom, we began to think Bull's discretion not so very extraordinary.[174]

Bull was a typical surface-loving dog, but Horace Hovey, a cave enthusiast who wrote several articles and books on Mammoth and other caves around the turn of the century, met a genuine cave dog on a visit to the cave in the 1870s.

Hovey wrote that two dogs lived at the Mammoth Cave Hotel. Jack, the older dog, would eagerly follow the guides and tourists to the gate at the cave entrance, but when all the lanterns disappeared into the darkness, Jack would return to the safety of the hotel where he could hobnob with visitors in the daylight.

There was also a pup, which the cave guides called Brigham, "'cause he's so young, you know!" explained Hovey's guide, William Bransford. Brigham happily followed tour groups into the dark cave.

Hovey said he and Brigham "became fast friends" during his two-week stay at the cave. The manager of the cave, Francis Klett, was also fond of the pup, and warned Hovey and the guides to not lose Brigham in the cave, fearing the dog would not be able to find his way out.

Brigham went with Hovey and Bransford on several cave trips. One day the three boated across the underground Echo River to the far reaches of the cave. On the far side of the river, Brigham spied a cave rat to chase. When the dog did not return from the chase, Bransford and Hovey called and whistled for him, but the only response was an echo. Brigham was lost! They had to return to the surface, so Bransford lit a lantern and set it on a ledge by Echo River so if Brigham found his way to the river he would have some light.

When Bransford and Hovey returned to the Mammoth Cave Hotel without Brigham, the visitors and employees were quite worried about the poor pup spending the night alone in the cave.

Brigham was not the only dog who enjoyed tagging along on cave tours. This 1857 sketch by Joachim Ferdinand Richardt shows a dog going for a boat ride on Echo River.

Brigham managed to find his way to Echo River, where he met a tour group the next morning. The relieved guide brought Brigham into the boat, soothed the rescued pup with kind words and hugs, and began the trip back across the river. But as soon as the boat reached the bank, Brigham made a getaway. The tour group, displeased with Brigham's lack of gratitude, returned to the surface without him.

The next day, Jack, the old dog, was also gone. The guides and visitors had to walk to the cave dogless. But when they got to the cave gate, there was Jack on the outside happily socializing with Brigham behind the bars. Amazed that Brigham used his nose to follow their scent more than a mile past cliffs and rocky crags in total darkness, Hovey and the group followed Brigham's paw prints. Brigham had not retraced the same route he went in, he followed the tour group's path out—the freshest scent. The tour group had returned from the river through a passage appropriately named the Corkscrew—shorter, but much rougher, than the route they took into the cave. There were three ladders to climb in the Corkscrew, tough enough if you have two hands and a lantern, tougher for a dog in the dark.[175]

The top of the Corkscrew.

Impressed with Brigham's caving and navigating skills, Horace Hovey wrote:

We honored him as a hero, and obtained for him, from the manager, Mr. Fancis Klett, the freedom of the cave for the rest of his life.

The Corkscrew was a tough climb for humans and canines alike. A tower built in Mammoth Dome in the 1950s eliminated the need to scramble up rocks and ladders through the Corkscrew.

Most cave explorers are human rather than canine. Volunteer cavers do the modern exploration in Mammoth Cave (no pups allowed). In the 1800s, the guides did most of the exploration. A British tourist named F. J. Stevenson joined cave guide and former slave

Nick Bransford to check out new cave passages in 1863. Stevenson's account of his cave adventure, "Adventures Underground, The Mammoth Cave of Kentucky in 1863," was published in *Blackwood's Magazine* in 1932.

After taking a cave tour, Stevenson relaxed at the hotel and listened to Mr. Owsley, the manager, tell of the only descent into a pit called the Maelstrom. Owsley said a "great avenue about halfway down" the pit was discovered, but it had not yet been explored. The regular tour route had not satisfied Stevenson's need for adventure, so he volunteered to be lowered down the pit to explore the new passage. Owsley ordered 300 feet of new rope from Louisville for the descent.

When Nick told Stevenson the Maelstrom was "heaps wuss" than Bottomless Pit, which they had crossed on the cave tour, Stevenson "began to feel a funny creeping sensation all up my backbone to the very roots of my hair ..." and hoped the rope would not arrive from Louisville or that something else would go wrong to stop the trip. But the rope arrived and about 30 curious people came to watch Stevenson's descent. Stevenson took a supply of Old Kentucky rye whisky into the cave for encouragement (this method of encouragement is not recommended).

The party hiked and boated about 5 miles into the cave to the Maelstrom. After a dinner of fried chicken and a dose of whisky, Stevenson had a twisty, dizzying descent down the new rope into the pit. Nick soon followed, having promised that he would accompany Stevenson down the pit. A new guide, a white man named Frank De Mowbrand (or Demunbrun), said that, "he was not going to be outdone by any — nigger in Kentucky," and followed them down the rope.

Stevenson claimed they went down "a wide and lofty avenue where no living creature had ever trod before." The passage came to a dead end, where he wrote "F. J. Stevenson of London, Eng., August 1863" in the sand.

The three were pulled back up on the rope. The party waiting for them at the top of the pit congratulated them and they began the trek out of the cave, Stevenson feeling better now that the Maelstrom was behind him.

When they arrived at the hotel, Owsley had a supper, fiddlers, and the neighbors waiting to hear their story. The manager admitted he had hoped for more exciting discoveries, but they still celebrated with food, singing, and dancing until the wee hours.

Stevenson also claimed to have explored a river that flowed at the bottom of Gorins Dome. Gorins Dome was included in some nineteenth century tours, but Stevenson ventured beyond the tour route. He had a special boat built, which Nick, Frank, and another guide helped carry to the river. Stevenson set out in the boat alone, though the guides insisted he tie a rope around his wrist so he would not get lost. Not wanting to be limited, Stevenson untied the rope once he was away from the guides. He had paddled far beyond earshot of the guides when he heard a terrifying sound, like a horse or large dog coughing. He doubted a surface animal could be that deep in the cave, but fired his revolver to warn whatever coughing creature was lurking in the dark. Apparently unfazed by the echoing gunshot, the creature coughed even more. Stevenson eventually discovered the "coughing" was an echo made by rippling water beating into a hole in the side of a passage. Stevenson wrote that he:

> ... felt a little disappointed that I had not encountered some monstrous, slimy water lizard, that I might have slain him and brought him out to daylight in triumph to astonish the whole scientific world with my discovery.

The next day Nick and Stevenson set out for a second adventure in the boat on the river in Gorins Dome. The little boat almost capsized with the weight of both of them, so Stevenson left Nick to wait for him on the bank. Stevenson wrote:

> Nick grumbled a good deal at being left there all alone, and I was hardly round a corner and out of his sight before I heard the poor fellow bawling to me for pity's sake to go back and fetch him off. ... It was about an hour and a half before I got back to where I had left Nick, and my conscience reproached me for deserting him so long. I found the poor fellow in a dreadful way. He had made up his mind that I had met with an accident and that he would be left alone to die in the darkness. He was crying like a child when I took him aboard, and he swore he would go no more with me on voyages of discovery for love nor money.[177]

Stevenson probably embellished his experiences to make himself appear to be an adventurous discoverer rather than the mere tourist that he was. It is unlikely that Nick, who had been working at Mammoth Cave for over 25 years, would cry in fear if left alone in the cave or allow an inexperienced visitor to take off exploring alone.

Stevenson called this river the Lost River because he did not know where the water originated or exited the cave. Today, it is called Stevensons Lost River because modern cave explorers can not find it—it does not exist. There is just a small pool at the bottom of Gorins Dome where Stevenson claimed to have found the river.

Cave jokes, the lowest form of humor (bad pun), are a long tradition with cave guides. Some of the corny jokes told on modern cave tours go back to the 1800s. In 1870, W. Stump Forwood, author of *An Historical and Descriptive Narrative of the Mammoth Cave of Kentucky,* heard a story at a cave formation called the Altar (a.k.a. the Bridal Altar) in Mammoth Cave's Gothic Avenue.

It is said that the fair lady, whose lover was opposed by her parents, in a rash moment promised them that she would never marry her betrothed on the face of the earth. Afterward, repenting her promise, but being unable to retract, and unwilling to violate it, she fulfilled her vow to her parents, as well as to her lover, by marrying him under the earth.[178]

A subterranean wedding at the Bridal Altar. Notice the guide with his torch throwing stick on the left.

A newspaper article from the October 15, 1936, edition of the *Franklin Favorite* told about an elderly woman who heard the same story on a cave tour. She stepped forward and claimed that she and three friends were married in a double ceremony at the Bridal Altar in the cave in 1879 and that one of the brides (she did not say which) had made the vow to "never marry any man on the top side of the earth and Mammoth Cave offered the solution."[179] The woman may have been wed in the cave, but the old joke predates her wedding by at least nine years.

Even though this story is probably a tale rather than historic fact, weddings did take place in Mammoth Cave in the late 1880s and early 1900s. Now that Mammoth Cave is a national park, weddings are no longer performed in the cave; the government does not want to be accused of running marriage into the ground. (Sorry, really)

A well-to-do couple was married at the Bridal Altar in 1882. The wedding party arrived by stage coach at the Mammoth Cave Hotel and said they wanted to have a wedding in the cave. Eager to please their guests, hotel employees ran to prepare the cave for the event. The 16-year-old bride had a fine silk dress "made in Louisville by the most artistic French milliner," but she was talked out of wearing her finery into the cave.[180]

The Bridal Altar was the most popular place to hold weddings in the cave, but an 1881 *New York Times* article told about a determined bride and groom who traveled 9 miles into the cave, with "the bride crawling hands and knees along the tunnel ..." and crossing an underground river to get to the desired place where "under nature's glittering gems, with darkness filling the depth beyond, and torches weirdly lighting the immediate space, the clergyman did his duty."[181]

Why would couples go the trouble of trekking into the cave to get married when it would have been easier and the brides' dresses would have remained much cleaner above ground? A newspaper article titled "Marriage in the Depths" attributed the desire to get married in Mammoth Cave and other unusual places to "the uneasy craving for novelty which marks the modern spirit. Perhaps it is only another evidence of that widespread reluctance to marry at all, which statisticians tell us is characteristic of the age. ..." The writer called this regrettable tendency part of "the same vulgar sensationalism which makes marriage, in what is called fashionable society, seem an undesirable thing. ..." He feared that, "mankind will probably lapse into universal celibacy, from lack of sufficiently novel holes and corners to get married in."[182] The words are typical of a person longing for the good old days before the younger generation ruined everything. The writer was lamenting about those crazy kids in 1870.

A coffin-shaped boulder appropriately named Giant's Coffin has the name "J.N. McDowell M.D. 1839," along with other graffiti from bygone days, scratched on it. Many visitors in the 1800s carved or smoked their names onto the cave walls as a record that they were there. (1800s graffiti is called "historic"; new graffiti is called "a misdemeanor.") Most of the names on the rock walls were written by long-forgotten travelers who disappeared into history.

Cave guides and visitors liked to look for shapes in the rocks, sort of like looking at the clouds or stars. With imagination, this big rock is a Giant's Coffin.

J.N. McDowell was one of the few who is famous enough to remember. People in the medical field know McDowell as the physician who founded the Washington University School of Medicine in St. Louis, Missouri. Guides at Mammoth Cave know him as an eccentric kook (though a smart kook). Story has it, Dr. McDowell became sick and thought he was dying. He called his medical partner and his son to his side and had them vow that when he died they would place his body in an alcohol-filled copper vase (or lead coffin, depending on which version of the story you read) and have it suspended from the roof of Mammoth Cave. Dr. McDowell claimed he had already made plans for his unusual entombment with the cave manager.

McDowell supposedly had the same plan for his daughter's burial; not in Mammoth Cave, but in a cave on his property in Hannibal, Missouri. Called McDowells Cave, the cave was popular with the local kids, including the young Mark Twain. Twain wrote about the cave (changing the name to McDougals Cave) in *The Adventures of Tom Sawyer* and mentioned McDowell's daughter's fate in his book *Life on the Mississippi.*

> In my time the person who owned it turned it into a mausoleum for his daughter, aged fourteen. The body of this poor child was put into a copper cylinder filled with alcohol, and this was suspended in one of the dismal avenues in the cave. The top of the cylinder was removable; and it was said to be a common thing for the baser order of tourists to drag the dead face into view and examine it and comment on it.[183]

Dr. McDowell was just the kind of person you might expect to do such a thing. He supposedly wore armor and had a cannon at his medical school because he feared being attacked by Catholics, claimed to see his mother's ghost while hiding among corpses, and had plans to invade and conquer Northern California—he was an odd guy.[184] But in spite of his credentials as a genuine eccentric, there is no solid evidence for his weird cave burial plans. McDowell's will does not mention his request to be entombed in Mammoth Cave. The earliest reference to the alcohol-filled-coffin story is an article in a 1908 edition of *The Medical Fortnightly*, published 40 years after he died. As for McDowell's daughter's body in McDowells Cave,* the owner of the cave in the 1990s vowed the story was true, but a Hannibal historian said he could find no proof of it. So do not look for Dr. McDowell's suspended body in Mammoth Cave, just his signature.

In 1881, a Frenchmen named Mazeller approached Francis Klett, the manager of Mammoth Cave, with an unusual idea. Mazeller, who was in the mushroom business in New York City, claimed it was hard to find large cellars with the right temperature and humidity to

---

* McDowells Cave in Hannibal is a show cave, open to the public. It is now called Mark Twain Cave, the famous author's name attracts more visitors than the eccentric doctor's name.

grow mushrooms near New York. Because mushrooms are a fungus, not a plant, they do not need light to grow. Mazeller felt Mammoth Cave was the perfect place for a mushroom farm.

French caves were already used to grow mushrooms. The French and other Europeans had become fans of the edible fungus, but few Americans saw mushrooms as food. Klett believed that there would be a market for this novel new food in Louisville or Cincinnati,[185] so he rented out space in Mammoth Cave's Vespertilio Hall. Raised beds were built for the mushrooms and underground mushroom farming began.

The mushroom business did not last long at the cave. Part of the problem may have been the difficulty of shipping the mushrooms to a market where someone would actually buy them. But the real problem was money. Klett claimed that Augustus Nicholson, one of the trustees who controlled the Mammoth Cave Estate, made him use the estate's money for the mushroom operation (it was a separate business from the hotel and cave). Nicholson called Klett a "scoundrel" and fired him.[186]

The mushroom beds are still in the cave, though not on a tour route.

A New Century

The twentieth century brought changes to Mammoth Cave, along with the rest of the world. Travelers began arriving in automobiles instead of the stage coach or train. Even the railroad, which had seemed so modern a generation earlier, was replaced with cars by 1929. Visitors could have their photos taken at the cave entrance and purchase the developed pictures when they returned from their tour. Electric lights eventually replaced the long-familiar lanterns in the cave. But perhaps the biggest change at the cave was the change of ownership.

The cave has had several owners over the years, but with the new century came a new owner who was not a private individual or family. Mammoth Cave became one of the first national parks east of the Mississippi River, making it the property of all American people.

The idea that the cave was worthy of being a national park came up as early as the turn of the century. A 1936 article in the Louisville *Courier-Journal* said that Milton Smith, president of the L&N Railroad, had proposed making Mammoth Cave a national park 35 years earlier.[187] The L&N Railroad ran through Cave City and Glasgow Junction (now called Park City) carrying travelers destined for the cave, so the railroad's interest in increasing the cave's popularity is not surprising.

About 1905, former Attorney General of Kentucky, M.M. Logan, suggested to Congressman James M. Richardson that Mammoth Cave be made a national park. Richardson said the Secretary of the Interior liked the idea (the National Parks are part of the Department of the Interior). If public interest could be drummed up, Richardson planned to introduce a bill to have the park created. Richardson was not re-elected, so the bill did not come to be.[188]

The concept of trying to make Mammoth Cave a national park caught on, though it took a while to get anywhere. In 1910, Richardson's successor, Congressman R.Y. Thomas, announced that he would introduce a bill in the next congress for the purchase of Mammoth Cave as a national park or forest reserve, but the bill failed.[189] Another congressman tried unsuccessfully to introduce a similar bill in 1912.[190]

Not everyone was interested in making the cave into a national park. An entrepreneur named George Morrison arrived at the cave hoping to have his own business. In 1916, Morrison learned that Mammoth Cave continued beyond the boundary of Mammoth Cave Estate, the part of the cave shown in the 1800s.

Morrison attempted to open his own show cave by blasting what he called the New Entrance to Mammoth Cave on land called the W.P. Cox tract. He surveyed and mapped passages leading from his New Entrance to the Mammoth Cave Estate, owned by the heirs of John Croghan, who had purchased the cave in the 1830s. To further prove it was all one cave, Morrison had some Mammoth Cave guides enter the Historic Entrance (at that time the only accepted entrance to the cave) and go out through his New Entrance.

Morrison's plan to profit from the cave was temporarily foiled when the Colossal Cavern Company (another show cave business), which owned the underground rights on the Cox tract, would not sell their cave rights or cooperate with Morrison.

Not one to give up, Morrison returned to the Mammoth Cave area in 1921. This time he managed to buy the cave rights to sections of Mammoth Cave beyond the land owned by Mammoth Cave Estate. He blasted a newer new entrance, which he again called the New Entrance. It is still called that today, in spite of it no longer being new. Morrison's first New Entrance is now called the Cox Entrance.[191]

Understandably, the trustees of Mammoth Cave Estate did not want to share the Mammoth Cave name or their customers with Morrison and his New Entrance. The Estate admitted that the New Entrance was connected "by a narrow and devious passage" with Mammoth Cave, but claimed Morrison's section of cave was "not 'Mammoth Cave' or any part thereof." The competition between the Estate and Morrison was vicious. The Mammoth Cave Estate trustees claimed Morrison had instructed his employees to threaten and beat up Estate employees to prevent them from luring customers to the old entrance of the cave and that Morrison paid any legal fines that resulted from these fights. Morrison denied using violence.[192] Mammoth Cave Estate published a pamphlet called *What the*

Mammoth Cave Guides Have to Say About the Pretended "New Entrance" Four Miles East from Green River. The pamphlet included several cave guides' signed statements saying they had never shown any areas in the New Entrance, and that the entrance on Mammoth Cave Estate was the only real entrance to the cave.[193]

The case went to court in 1926. Judge Chas. I. Dawson ruled that Morrison could use the name "New Entrance to Mammoth Cave," but ads and verbal descriptions of the New Entrance had to include this cautionary phrase to avoid misleading the public:

> We do not show any of that part of the cave which, prior to 1907, was generally known to the public as "Mammoth Cave." That portion of the Cave can be seen only through the old Entrance.[194]

Morrison did not have long to enjoy his New Entrance to Mammoth Cave. Permanent changes were underway.

The push to make Mammoth Cave into a national park really started to move in 1924 with the creation of the Mammoth Cave National Park Committee, which became the Mammoth Cave National Park Association. The Association generated public interest with meetings, advertising, and a membership drive. An ad told readers:

> Your membership in the Mammoth Cave National Park Association will help to save Mammoth Cave for all our country. ... Its membership is composed of men and women from many states who believe that there should be established more national parks in the East—and especially a national park in the Mammoth Cave region, in order to preserve for all people for all time one of the greatest of the natural wonders of the world.
>
> Interested citizens of the United States are invited to become members of the Mammoth Cave National Park Association and, through their membership fee of $1.00, make possible the organized presentation of a plan for Congressional action.[195]

The Association's efforts paid off. In April 1926, Congressman M.L. Thatcher introduced legislation to make the cave a national park and Senator Richard P. Ernst introduced the bill in the Senate. President Calvin Coolidge signed it that May.[196]

Not everyone was happy to see the creation of Mammoth Cave National Park. The legislation stated that at least 45,310 acres had to be acquired for the area to become a national park.[197] That meant the acquisition of not only the cave entrances and the land immediately around them controlled by Mammoth Cave Estate and George Morrison, but land belonging to nearly 600 families in the area. Understandably, some people did not want to sell their land. In 1928, the Kentucky National Park Commission was set up with the power of eminent domain, which means the ability to purchase land for public use whether the owner wants to sell or not.

Dr. Croghan stated in his will in 1848 that when all nine of his nieces and nephews who inherited Mammoth Cave Estate had died, the property was to be sold at public sale. Croghan's last niece, Serena Croghan Rogers, died in August, 1926.[198] The Mammoth Cave National Park Association was able to buy two-thirds interest in the Estate for $446,000, but one-third interest was controlled by an heir's offspring who did not want to sell. That third was purchased through eminent domain.[199] George Morrison's New Entrance to Mammoth Cave was purchased for $290,000 in 1932.[200]

Most of the families who had to sell their land lived in Edmonson County. The *Edmonson County News* printed several negative articles about the creation of the new park. A February 26, 1931, article compared the plight of local land owners to that of American Indians.

> To Hell with the National Park ... We find in the Kentucky History where Elsquawater and Ficheamsha, two great Indian chiefs and fighters and dear lovers of Old Kentucky, our happy hunting grounds. But they were driven out and had to leave their happy hunting ground. I wonder who will be to blame if we have to leave our happy hunting ground, it won't be Daniel Boone and Simon Kenton.[201]

Today, the National Park Service tends to have a good relationship with park neighbors, but understandably some people still have negative or mixed feelings about the park. Edmonson County native George McCombs, who was a small child when his family had to sell their land for the creation of the park, shared his view.

> I'm crazy about Mammoth Cave, but another part of me still dislikes it. I was born at Joppa. There was an old high school across

the road. My dad taught school up there. He told me stories about when they first got ready to buy the park that officials—I don't know if it was somebody local who was hired or appointed, or officials from Washington—would come to the schools and talk to all the little kids. They'd tell them what wonderful things they were going to do with Mammoth Cave. They were going to build this beautiful place, there was going to be recreation for everybody, there's going to be jobs for all your fathers, your brothers, and your uncles, they'd make good money. Then they'd take up a collection from the little kids to help pay for the park. My dad hated that so much. Then when the park was formed, people from Edmonson County got pushed aside.[202]

Mammoth Cave's transformation to a full-fledged national park was gradual. In 1936, the cave was given the status of a national park, but it received no government funding until 1941, when the National Park Service completely took responsibility for its administration and protection. In 1946, about 45 years after talk first began, the formal dedication took place.[203]

This is what cavers must endure to explore new passages.
Photograph by Rick Olson.

Another great event for Mammoth Cave in the twentieth century was a confirmation of what people already believed. The cave had long been touted as the longest cave in the world—cave guides claimed it was 150 (or 300, or 600) miles long since the 1800s. Exaggerations became reality on September 9, 1972.

Prior to that date, nearly 58 miles had been surveyed in Mammoth Cave; nearby Flint Ridge Cave had 86 miles surveyed. For years, cave explorers suspected the two caves were connected, but no connecting passage had been found. In August, 1972, cavers were exploring a virgin passage in Flint Ridge Cave when they spotted an arrow and the name "Pete H" scratched in the mud on the cave wall. If you are in virgin cave passage and you see a name, it tells you either the bats are smarter than you thought or you're not really the first person there. The explorers knew who had left his signature—Pete Hanson, a guide and explorer at Mammoth Cave in the 1930s. Had Pete got to that point in Flint Ridge Cave through Mammoth Cave or had he entered through an entrance that was unknown to the explorers in 1972? The cavers were tired, wet, and cold, but the exciting thought of finding a passage connecting to Mammoth Cave made them decide to explore for one more hour.

An hour later, they were exhausted and still had not found a connection. They mustered up enough energy for the 5½-mile trip back to the cave entrance, planning to come back later to explore further.

The next month, the explorers were back in Flint Ridge Cave for another long, wet, exhausting trip. They passed the Pete H signature and reached a water-filled passage that had only a foot of space between the water and the ceiling; it did not look good. John Wilcox, the leader of the expedition, went ahead to see if it was possible to continue, no use everyone getting completely soaked. John expected that he would have to turn around, but the passage soon opened into a bigger room. As he looked around, his light reflected off of a horizontal line—a handrail. "I see a tourist trail!" he shouted back to his pals, knowing they had reached Mammoth Cave. They made the most important connection in caving history, making the Flint-Mammoth Cave System 144 miles long—by far the longest in the world. The trip out of the cave was much easier than the trip in. Instead of wading, crawling, stooping, and climbing several miles, the explorers emerged from Echo River and walked on a smooth tour trail about 2 miles to the Snowball Room, where a phone and elevator were waiting. They called the Chief Ranger and had him radio the ranger on night duty to pick them up at the top of the elevator.[204]

The tour trail that John Wilcox saw as he came out of the water filled passage had been used by tours since the mid 1800s (though it has not been used since the 1960s). How did over 100 years of guides, tourists, and explorers miss the connecting passage? Usually, the water in Echo River blocks the passage, making it look more like a dent in the rock than a separate passage. September, 1972, was the end of a dry summer; the water level was lower than usual, making it possible to wade through an area that was usually full of water.

Mammoth Cave has attracted international travelers since tours began, but by the twentieth century, airplanes and cars made the world smaller, making it easier to reach rural Kentucky. Mammoth Cave became recognized as valuable not only nationally, but world wide. In 1981, the United Nations Educational Scientific and Cultural Organization (UNESCO) designated Mammoth Cave as a World Heritage Site. World Heritage Sites usually receive this designation because of their cultural importance, like the Great Wall of China and Taj Mahal. Mammoth Cave was recognized mostly for its significance as the longest cave in the world, along with its rich archeology and history.[205]

The Mammoth Cave area received additional international significance when UNESCO designated it an International Biosphere Reserve in 1990. Sites designated as Biosphere Reserves are exemplary natural environments. Yellowstone National Park and Brazil's Central Amazon are among other Biosphere Reserves.

Though these titles were granted by the United Nations, Mammoth Cave does not belong to, nor is it controlled by the United Nations. Being designated a World Heritage Site and an International Biosphere Reserve gives Mammoth Cave extra recognition and prestige, but it does not change the ownership.

The twenty-first century will undoubtedly bring more changes. A lot has changed since the first visitors toured Mammoth Cave two centuries ago, but people are still drawn to the cave for the same reasons. It will always be a place of wonder, mystery, discovery, and adventure.

Notes

1 Kohl, Johann Georg, 1857. "Excerpt from Johann Georg Kohl's Travels in the Northwest of the United States," *The Journal of Spelean History*, January–March, 1990, p 3.

2 Taylor, Bayard, 1855. *At Home and Abroad*, p 193.

3 Hall, Frederick, 1840. *Letters From the East and From the West,* p 142.

4 Shackleford, Oliver, 1920. "History of Cave," p 4.

5 Ward, John, 1854. John Ward Diary for May–July, 1854.

6 "My Gropings Nine Miles Under Ground," *The National Magazine,* circa 1855, p 58.

7 Staurt-Wortley, Eaimeline, 1851. *Travels in the United States, Etc.* New York: Harper & Brothers.

8 "Bell's Tavern," *The Glasgow Weekly Times*, February 13, 1895, p 1.

9 Gardiner, Florence Edwards, 1940. *Cyrus Edwards' Stories of Early Days and Others*. Louisville: The Standard Printing Company, p 225.

10 Willis, Nathaniel Parker, 1853. *Health Trip to the Tropics*. New York: Charles Scribner, pp 146-149.

11 Gardiner, Florence Edwards, 1940. Cyrus Edwards' Stories of Early Days and Others. Louisville: The Standard Printing Company, pp 226–228.

12 *Glasgow Weekly Times*, December 4, 1879, p3.

13 Tissandier, Albert, 1885. "Six Months in the United States." Translated by Mary F. Francey. Collection of the Utah Museum of Fine Arts.

14 Wells, R.L., 1869. "A Visit to Mammoth Cave," *The Journal of Proceedings of the Illinois State Teachers' Association* at its Fifteenth Annual Meeting, Held in Peoria, Dec. 29, 1868. Peoria: Office of the Illinois Teacher, p 123.

15 Measuring Worth—Relative Value of U.S. Dollars Web site, http://www.measuringworth.com.

16 Ward, John, 1854. John Ward Diary for May–July 1854.

17 Zagel, Hermann, 1887. "An Excursion to Mammoth Cave in Kentucky" *Die Abendschule. Ein Familienblatt*, Vol. 34, 1888, p 556.

18 Ward, John, 1854. John Ward Diary for May–July 1854.

19 Hovey, H.C., 1880. *One Hundred Miles in Mammoth Cave*–In 1880. Reprint, 1982, Golden, Colorado: Outbooks, p 3.

20 Gollar, C. Walker, 1995. "The Mammoth Cave Stagecoach Robbery and the Effectiveness of the Kentucky Judicial System in the 1880s," *The Filson Club Quarterly*, October, 1995, pp 347–364.

21 Harlow, Alvin F. *Weep No More, My Lady*. New York: Whttlesey House, p 269.

22 Gollar, C. Walker, 1995. "The Mammoth Cave Stagecoach Robbery and the Effectiveness of the Kentucky Judicial System in the 1880s," *The Filson Club History Quarterly*, October, 1995, pp 347–364.

23 Dickey, Earle, 1937. "Cave City, Gateway to Kentucky's Cave Region," The *Louisville & Nashville Employes'* [*sic*] *Magazine*, November, 1937, p 13.

24 Sulzer, Elmer G. 1958. "The Mammoth Cave Railroad," *Railway and Locomotive Historical Society Bulletin*, No. 990, pp 32–33, 35, 37, 39.

25 Thompson, Ralph Seymour, 1879. *The Sucker's Visit to The Mammoth Cave*. Springfield, Ohio: Live Patron Publishing Office. Reprinted 1970, New York: Johnson Reprint Corporation, pp126–127.

26 Shackleford, Oliver P, 1920. "An Account of the History of Mammoth Cave During the Middle Nineteenth Century by Oliver Shackleford, One of the Guides." Unpublished interview. pp 2–3.

27 Croghan, John, 1839. A letter to General T. S. Jesup Library of Congress microfilm (R-2).

28 Hall, Frederick, 1840. *Letters From the East and From the West*. Washington: F. Taylor and Wm. M. Morrison, p 143.

29 Gard, S.L., 1853. A letter. Mammoth Cave National Park manuscript collection.

30 Burleson, Rufus C., 1859. *Biography and Letters of Dr. Rufus C. Burleson*. pp 293–294.

31 Underwood, J.R., 1862. "Report of affairs at the 'Mammoth Cave' for the year 1861."

32 Frank, 1862. Batchelor-Turner Letters 186–1862, Annotated by H.J.H. Rugeley.

33 Ferguson, Robert, 1866. *America During and After the War*. London: Longmans, Green, Reader, and Dyer, p 138.

34 Forwood, W. Stump, 1870. *An Historical and Descriptive Narrative of the Mammoth Cave of Kentucky*. Philadelphia: J.B. Lippincott & Co.,

pp 37–38.

35 Graves, D.L., 1872.Newspaper advertisement, Mammoth Cave National Park manuscript collection.

36 Hovey, Horace Carter, 1896. *Celebrated American Caves.* Cincinnati: Robert Clarke & Co. Reprinted 1970, New York: Johnson Reprint Corporation, pp 67–68.

37 Tissandier, Albert, 1885. *Six Months in the United States.*

38 Zagel, Hermann, 1887. "An Excursion to the Mammoth Cave in Kentucky." Reprinted in an article by Richard A. Weiss in *Register: Kentucky Historical Society*, Vol. 71, No. 3, July 1973, p 276.

39 Morgan, M. C., Reminiscences of Mammoth Cave. Mammoth Cave National Park Manuscript Collection.

40 Hovey, H.C., 1880. *One Hundred Miles in Mammoth Cave–In 1880.* Reprinted in 1982. Golden, Colorado: Outbooks, p 11.

41 Wright, Charles W., 1860. *A Guide Manual to the Mammoth Cave of Kentucky.* Louisville: Bradley & Gilbert, p 26.

42 Procter, John R., 1898. "The Mammoth Cave of Kentucky," *The Century Magazine*, Vol. LV, March, 1898, p 650.

43 Stevenson, F.J. "Adventures Underground. The Mammoth Cave of Kentucky in 1863." *Blackwood's Magazine*, June, 1932, p 733.

44 Morgan, M. C. Reminiscences of Mammoth Cave. Mammoth Cave National Park Manuscript Collection.

45 Thompson, Ralph Seymour, 1879. *The Sucker's Visit to The Mammoth Cave.* Springfield, Ohio: Live Patron Publishing Office. Reprinted 1970, New York: Johnson Reprint Corporation, p 75.

46 Myers, Robert Manson, 1972. *The Children of Pride, A True story of Georgia and the Civil War.* p 73.

47 "The Underground Territories of the United States," *The International Magazine of Literature, Art, and Science*, Vol. V., No. 1, January 1, 1852.

48 Zagel, Hermann, 1887. An Excursion to the Mammoth Cave in Kentucky. Reprinted in an article by Richard A. Weiss in *Register: Kentucky Historical Society.* Vol. 71, No. 3, July 1973, p 277.

49 Bird, Robert Montgomery, 1838. *Peter Pilgrim: or A Rambler's Recollections.* Philadelphia: Lea & Blanchard, p 80.

50 Binkerd, A.D., 1869. *The Mammoth Cave And its Denizens: A Complete Descriptive Guide.* Cincinnati: Robert Clarke & Co., p 23.

51 Meriam, Ebenezer, 1844. "Mammoth Cave," *New York Municipal Gazette*, February 21, 1844, pp 320–321.

52 Williams, C. Foster, circa 1882. *Sermon in the Mammoth Cave.*

53 Anonymous, 1810. *The Subterranean Voyage, or The Mammoth Cave,*

Partially Explored.

54 Bird, Robert Montgomery, 1838. *Peter Pilgrim: or A Rambler's Recollections.* Philadelphia: Lea & Blanchard, pp 117–119.

55 Gard, S.L., 1853. An unpublished letter, Mammoth Cave National Park Manuscript Collection.

56 "United States Circuit Court of Appeals, Sixth Circuit. Transcript of Record, Wyatt and Janin vs. Mammoth Cave Development Company." 1927, p 7.

57 Eyth, Max, 1867. "How I Have Celebrated Christmas In The Mammoth Cave," Mammoth Cave National Park Manuscript Collection.

58 *Ibid.*

59 Erwin, Joseph Warner, 1852. A journal entry, Mammoth Cave National Park Manuscript Collection.

60 Anonymous, circa 1848. "Reminiscences of a Trip Through Mammoth Cave," Mammoth Cave National Park Manuscript Collection.

61 Hovey, Horace Carter, 1896. *Celebrated American Caverns.* Cincinnati: Robert Clarke & Co. Reprinted 1970, New York: Johnson Reprint Company, p 79.

62 Anonymous, 1852. "The Underground Territories of the United States," *The International Magazine of Literature, Art, and Science.* January 1, 1852, p 10.

63 Thompson, Ralph Seymour, 1879. *The Sucker's Visit to The Mammoth Cave.* Springfield, Ohio: Live Patron Publishing Office. Reprinted 1970, New York: Johnson Reprint Corporation, pp 89–91.

64 Bird, Robert Montgomery, 1838. *Peter Pilgrim: or A Rambler's Recollections.* Philadelphia: Lea & Blanchard, p 135.

65 Wright, Charles W., M.D., 1860. *A Guide Manual to the Mammoth Cave of Kentucky.* Louisville: Bradley & Gilbert, pp 44–45.

66 Hovey, H.C., 1880. *One Hundred Miles in Mammoth Cave.* Reprinted 1982, Golden, Colorado: Outbooks, p 23.

67 Kirchhoff, Theodor, 1870. "Mammoth Cave Through a German's Eyes: A Visit by Theodore Kirchhoff in 1870." Translated by Frederick Trautmann, *Register of the Kentucky Historical Society*, Autumn, 1983, p 392.

68 Anonymous, 1852. "The Underground Territories of the United States." *The International Magazine of Literature, Art, and Science.* January 1, 1852, p 24.

69 Burleson, Rufus C., 1859. Biography and Letters of Dr. Rufus C. Burleson, p 294.

70 *Ibid.*
71 Wortley, Emmeline Stuart, 1851. *Travels in the U.S., Etc. During 1849 and 1850.* New York: Harper & Brothers, pp 177–178.
72 Hovey, Horace Carter, 1896. *Celebrated American Caverns.* Cincinnati: Robert Clarke & Co. Reprinted 1970, New York: Johnson Reprint Corporation, p 105.
73 Anonymous, 1961. "A Tour in the Mammoth Cave," *All the Year Round*, January 19, 1861, p 346.
74 Erwin, Joseph Warner, 1852. A journal from 1839–1853. Mammoth Cave National Park Manuscript Collection.
75 Zagel, Hermann, 1887. "An Excursion to Mammoth Cave in Kentucky", translated by Richard A. Weiss in *Register:Kentucky Historical Society*, July, 1973, pp 285–286,
76 Thompson, Ralph Seymour, 1879. *The Sucker's Visit to The Mammoth Cave.* Springfield, Ohio: Live Patron Publishing Office. Reprinted 1970, New York: Johnson Reprint Corporation, p 104.
77 Zagel, Hermann, 1887. "An Excursion to Mammoth Cave in Kentucky," translated by Richard A. Weiss in *Register: Kentucky Historical Society*, July, 1973, p 285.
78 Wells, E.L., 1869, "The Journal of Proceedings of the Illinois State Teachers' Association," Peoria, Illinois: Office of the Illinois Teacher, p 130.
79 Thompson, Ralph Seymour, 1879. *The Sucker's Visit to The Mammoth Cave.* Springfield, Ohio: Live Patron Publishing Office. Reprinted 1970, New York: Johnson Reprint Corporation, p 111.
80 Anonymous, 1843. "Journal of a Trip Through Kentucky and a Visit to Mammoth Cave." Mammoth Cave National Park Manuscript Collection.
81 Anonymous, 1852. "The Underground Territories of the United States," *The International Magazine of Literature, Art, and Science,* January 1, 1852, p 27.
82 Stevenson, F.J., 1863. "Adventures Underground. The Mammoth Cave of Kentucky in 1863," *Blackwood's Magazine*, June, 1932, pp 739–740.
83 Zagel, Hermann, 1887. "An Excursion to Mammoth Cave in Kentucky", translated by Richard A. Weiss in *Register: Kentucky Historical Society,* July, 1973, p 289.
84 Thompson, Ralph Seymour, 1879. *The Sucker's Visit to The Mammoth Cave.* Springfield, Ohio: Live Patron Publishing Office. Reprinted 1970, New York: Johnson Reprint Corporation, p 114.
85 Hovey, H.C., 1880. *One Hundred Miles in Mammoth Cave.* Reprinted

1982, Golden, Colorado: Outbooks, p 23.

86 Stevenson, F.J., "Adventures Underground. The Mammoth Cave of Kentucky in 1863," *Blackwood's Magazine*, June, 1932, p 724.

87 Kerchhoff, Theodore. "Mammoth Cave Through a German's Eyes: A Visit by Theodor Kirchhoff in 1870," Translated by Frederic Trautmann, *Register of the Kentucky Historical Society*, Autumn, 1983, p 386.

88 Wortley, Emeline Stuart, 1851. *Travels in the United States Etc. During 1849 and 1850.* New York: Harper & Brothers.

89 Haywood, John, 1853. "Mammoth Cave, Kentucky," *A Gazetteer of the United States of America.* Reprinted in The Journal of Spelean History, Jan.–March, 1981, p 4.

90 Thompson, Ralph Seymour, 1879. *The Sucker's Visit to The Mammoth Cave.* Springfield, Ohio: Live Patron Publishing Office. Reprinted 1970, New York; Johnson Reprint Corporation, p 117.

91 Anonymous, circa 1892. "Lost in the Mammoth Cave," *Chicago Mail.*

92 Taylor, Bayard, 1855. *At Home and Abroad.* p 205.

93 Finch, Marianne, 1853. *An Englishwoman's Experience in America.* London: Richard Bentley, p 351.

94 Davidson, R. 1840. *An Excursion to the Mammoth Cave, and the Barrens of Kentucky.* Lexington: A. T. Skillman & Son, p 66.

95 Forwood, W. Stump, 1870. *An Historical and Descriptive Narrative of the Mammoth Cave of Kentucky.* Philadelphia: J. B. Lippincott & Co., pp 25–26.

96 Meloy, Harold, 1978. "Dr. Call at Mammoth Cave," Mammoth Cave National Park Manuscript Collection.

97 Conner, Eugene H. and Samuel W. Thomas, 1966. *John Croghan, An Enterprising Kentucky Physician.* Louisville: University of Louisville, p 222.

98 DiBlasi, Philip, "The Enslaved Individuals Owned By the Croghans." Mammoth Cave National Park Manuscript Collection.

99 Lyons, Joy Medley, 2006. *Making Their Mark: The Signature of Slavery at Mammoth Cave.* Fort Washington, PA: Eastern National.

100 Kendall, Phebe Mitchell, 1896. *Maria Mitchell, Life, Letters and Journals.*

101 Galey, Thomas Mellon, 1951. An unpublished letter. Mammoth Cave National Park Manuscript Collection.

102 Slayton, Asa Walker, 1864. "Civil War Journal, 1862–1864," *Grand Rapids Weekly Eagle.*

103 Stevenson, F.J., 1932. "Adventures Underground. The Mammoth Cave of Kentucky in 1863," *Blackwood's Magazine*, June, 1932, pp

722–723, 747–748,

104 *Louisville Daily Journal*, August 20, 1863, p 3.

105 Lyons. Joy Medley, 2006. *Making Their Mark, the Signature of Slavery at Mammoth Cave*. Fort Washington, PA: Eastern National, p 51.

106 Lockard, Joe, 2002. "'A Light Broke Out Over My Mind' Mattie Griffith, Madge Vertner, and Kentucky Abolitionism," *The Filson History Quarterly*, Summer 2002, p 259.

107 Cigna, Arrigo A., 1997. "An Italian Traveller (sic) at Mammoth Cave in the 19th Century," *The Journal of Spelean History*, July–Sept 1997, p 59.

108 Ferguson, Robert, 1866. *America During and After the War*. London: Longmans, Green, Reader and Dyer, p 139.

109 Bird, Robert Montgomery, 1838, *Peter Pilgrim: or A Rambler's Recollections*. Philadelphia: Lea & Blanchard, p 110.

110 Traister, Daniel. "Robert Montgomery Bird: Writer and Artist," University of Pennsylvania Web site.

111 "The Life of Bayard Taylor 1825–1878," The Bayard Taylor Memorial Library Web site.

112 Taylor, Bayard, 1855. *At Home and Abroad*. p 214.

113 Willis, Nathaniel Parker, 1853. *Health Trip to the Tropics*. New York: Charles Scribner, pp 180–181.

114 "Nathaniel Parker Willis," Wikipedia Web site.

115 Emerson, Ralph Waldo. "Illusions," *Essays For Our Day*. Edited by Shackleford, L.B. and F.P Gass. New York: W.W. Norton & Company, Inc., pp 62–63.

116 Parish, Sam K. "The Great Hole in the Ground," *Glasgow Daily News*, June 3, 2000.

117 Melville, Herman, 1851. *Moby Dick*.

118 Verne, Jules, 1993. "A Journey to the Center of the Earth." *The Works of Jules Verne*, 1993. Stamford: Longmeadow Press, p 600.

119 Muir, John, 1991. *A Thousand-Mile Walk to the Gulf*. San Francisco: Sierra Club Books, p 7.

120 "Regis Francois Gignoux, (1816–1882)", The Lawrence J. Cantor & Company Fine Old Art Web site, http://www.fineoldart.com.

121 Thompson, Bob, 2002. "Historic Paintings of Mammoth Cave," *NSS News*, April, 2002, p 108.

122 Thompson, Bob, 2002. "Historic Paintings of Mammoth Cave," *NSS News*, April, 2002, p 109.

123 Science and Society Picture Library Web site, http://www.scienceandsociety.co.uk/results.asp?image=10216073.

124 Thompson, Bob, 2006. "Albert Tissandier's Drawings of Mammoth

Cave," *The Journal of Spelean History*, January–June 2006, pp 23–27.

125 Thompson, Bob, 2002. "Historic Paintings of Mammoth Cave," *NSS News*, April, 2002, p 110.

126 "Painting WKU's Kentucky Museum to be Displayed at U.S. Embassy in Latvia," a June 28, 2005, News Release from Western Kentucky University.

127 ViolinMan.com Web site, http://www.violinman.com

128 "Mammoth Cave" *Salem Register*, June 26, 1845, reprinted by Gurnee, Russel, 1983. News Clippins on Caves, 19th Century Newspapers, p 56.

129 "Jenny Lind." Mammoth Cave National Park Manuscript Collection.

130 "Jenny Lind." Mammoth Cave National Park Manuscript Collection.

131 "Edwin Booth." Wikipedia Web site.

132 Grossmann, Edwina Booth, *Edwin Booth, Recollections by His Daughter. New York: Benjamin Blom, pp 46–47.*

133 *Rafinesque, C. S., 1832.* "The Caves of Kentucky," *The Atlantic Journal,* Vol. 1, 1832. Reprinted 1975, *The Journal of Spelean History,* Jan.–March, 1975.

134 *Ibid.* p 7.

135 Streshinsky, Shirley, 1993. *Audubon, Life and Art in the American Wilderness.* New York: Villard Books, pp 94-95.

136 "Maria Mitchell," Distinguished Women Web site.

137 "Maria Mitchell," Mammoth Cave National Park manuscript collection.

138 Kliebhan, Bernd, 1999. "The Contribution of E. A. Martel (1859–1938) to the Development of Caving Technique." The Bernd Kliebhan Web site.

139 Miller, James Russell, "Pedro II, Emperor of Brazil," Historical Text Archive, http://historicaltextarchive.com.

140 Dickey, Earle, 1935. "Cave City, Gateway to Kentucky's Cave Region," The *Louisville & Nashville Employes [sic] Magazine,* November, 1935, pp 13–14.

141 "The Duke at the Cave," *Courier-Journal*, February 3, 1872.

142 "Royalty Underground," *Courier-Journal*, February 2, 1872.

143 Thompson, Bob, 2003. "Mammoth Cave Hotel Registers," *Journal of Spelean History*, Vol. 37, No. 1, Jan.–June 2003, pp 27, 32.

144 Thompson, Bob, 2003. "Mammoth Cave Hotel Registers," *Journal of Spelean History*, Vol. 37, No. 1, Jan.–June 2003, p 31.

145 Bird, Robert Montgomery, 1838. *Peter Pilgrim: or A Rambler's Recollections.* Philadelphia: Lea & Blanchard, p 109.

146 Meriam, Ebenezer, 1844. "Mammoth Cave," *New York Municipal Gazette*, February 21, 1844, p 319.

147 Sallee, Scott, 1997. "Tambo." Unpublished paper from the Mammoth Cave National Park manuscript collection. The letter from Miller is in the possession of Joseph S. Hays.

148 Finch, Marianne, 1853. *An Englishwoman's Experience in America.* London: Richard Bentley Publication in Ordinary to Her Majesty, p 340.

149 Wright, Charles W., 1860. *A Guide Manual to the Mammoth Cave.* Louisville: Bradley & Gilbert, p 9.

150 Hayward, John, 1853. *A Gazetteer of the United States of America.* Reprinted in *The Journal of Spelean History,* Jan.–March 1981, p 4.

151 Anonymous, 1852. "The Underground Territories of the United States," *The International Magazine of Literature, Art, and Science,* January 1, 1852, p 19.

152 Trautmann, Frederic, 1983. "Mammoth Cave Through a German's Eyes: a Visit by Theodor Kirchhoff in 1870," *Register of the Kentucky Historical Society,* Autumn, 1983, pp 389–390.

153 Wright, Charles W., 1860. *A Guide Manual to the Mammoth Cave.* Louisville: Bradley & Gilbert, p 9.

154 Vigne, Godfrey, T., 1832. *Six Months in America.* London: Whitaker, Treacher and Co. Reprinted 1833, Philadelphia: Thomas T. Ash, p 24.

155 Thompson, Ralph Seymour, 1879. *The Sucker's Visit to The Mammoth Cave.* Springfield: Live Patron Publishing Office. Reprinted 1970, New York: Johnson Reprint Corporation, p 116.

156 Croghan, John, 1839. A letter to General T.S. Jesup Library of Congress microfilm (R-2).

157 Taylor, Bayard, 1855. *At Home and Abroad.* p 200

158 Stevenson, F.J., 1932. "Adventures Underground. The Mammoth Cave of Kentucky in 1863," *Blackwood's Magazine,* June, 1932, pp 729-730.

159 Anderson, O.H.P, 1843. A letter to Henry Wingate, Esq., Frankfort, Kentucky, January 12, 1843. Mammoth Cave National Park Manuscript Collection.

160 Croghan, John, 1843. A letter to General T.S. Jesup, January 13, 1843. Library of Congress microfilm (R-1).

161 Martineau, Harriet, 1837. "Solitaires," *Society in America,* Volume I, PartII—Economy, (Section 1). London: Saunders and Otley, p 236.

162 Kennedy, Mary C. and Patty Jo Watson, 1997. "The Chronology of Early Agriculture and Intensive Mineral Mining in the Salts Cave and Mammoth Cave Region, Mammoth Cave National Park, Kentucky," *Journal of Cave and Karst Studies,* Vol. 59, p 5.

163 Benington, Frederick, Carl Melton, and Patty Jo Watson, 1962.

"Carbon Dating Prehistoric Soot from Salts Cave, Kentucky," *American Antiquity*, Vol. 28, p 241.

164 Watson, Patty Jo, 1969. *The Prehistory of Salts Cave Kentucky*. Springfield: State of Illinois, p 58.

165 Hovey, Horace, 1896. *Celebrated American Caves*. New York: Johnson Reprint Corporation, Reprint 1970, p 76.

166 Blane, William N., 1824. *Mammoth Cave Winter of 1822–1823 as Described by William N. Blane in An Excursion Through The United States and Canada*. London, p 272.

167 Wilkins, Charles, 1817. A letter to Samuel M. Burnside, Secretary of the American Antiquarian Society, *Transactions and Collections of the American Antiquarian Society*, vol. I (1820), pp 361–362.

168 Anonymous, 1814, "Green River, or Mammoth Cave," *Medical Repository* Vol. 17, 1815, pp 391–392.

169 Robbins, Louise M., 1974. "Prehistoric People of the Mammoth Cave Area," *Archeology of the Mammoth Cave Area*. Edited by Patty Jo Watson. St. Louis; Cave Books, Second Edition, 1997, p 145.

170 Watson, Patty Jo, 1974. "Observation and Recording in Salts Cave," *Archeology of the Mammoth Cave Area*. St. Louis: Cave Books, Reprint 1997, p 25.

171 Watson, Patty Jo, 1974. "Observation and Recording in Salts Cave," *Archeology of the Mammoth Cave Area*. St. Louis: Cave Books, Reprint 1997, pp 27–28.

172 Robinson, Louise M., 1974. "Prehistoric People of the Mammoth Cave Area," *Archeology of the Mammoth Cave Area*. Edited by Patty Jo Watson. St. Louis: Cave Books, Reprint 1997, pp 142–144.

173 Forwood, W. Stump, 1870. *An Historical and Descriptive Narrative of the Mammoth Cave of Kentucky*. Philadelphia: J. B. Lippincott & Co., p 34.

174 Bird, Robert Montgomery, 1838. *Peter Pilgrim: or a Rambler's Recollections*. Philadelphia: Lea & Blanchard, p 72.

175 Hovey, Horace, 1896. *Celebrated American Caverns*. New York: Johnson Reprint Corporation, Reprint 1970, pp 119–121.

176 Hovey, Horace, circa 1880. "Brigham, the Cave-Dog." Mammoth Cave National Park Manuscript Collection.

177 Stevenson, F.J., 1932. "Adventures Underground," *Blackwood's Magazine*, June, 1932, pp 742–747, 753–756.

178 Forwood, W. Stump, M.D. *An Historical and Descriptive Narrative of the Mammoth Cave of Kentucky*. Philadelphia: J. B. Lippincott & Co, p 202.

179 "Franklin Woman Visits Double Ceremony Scene," *Franklin Favorite,* October 15, 1936.

180 "A Sixteen-Year-Old Bride," *New York Times,* September 24, 1882.

181 "Married in the Mammoth Cave," *New York Times*, October 19, 1881, p 2.

182 "Marriage in the Depths," *New York Times*, August, 13, 1870, p 4.

183 Twain, Mark, 1883. *Life on the Mississippi.* Reprint, 1992, New York: Book-of-the-Month-Club, pp 451–452.

184 Brodman, Estelle, 1980. "The Great Eccentric," *Washington University Magazine*, December, 1980, pp 9–10.

185 Hovey, Horace Carter, 1881. "A Mushroom Farm in Mammoth Cave," *Scientific American*, June 11, 1881, p 369.

186 Croghan, George, 1903. "The Mammoth Cave Controversy," a Court Record. Michigan Bar, Sacramento County, California.

187 Goode, Cecil E., 1986. *World Wonder Saved, How Mammoth Cave Became a National Park.* Mammoth Cave, Kentucky: The Mammoth Cave National Park Association, p 20.

188 *Ibid.*

189 Anonymous, 1910. "A Neglected Natural Wonder," *The Courier-Journal*, October 29, 1910.

190 Goode, Cecil E., 1986. *World Wonder Saved, How Mammoth Cave Became a National Park.* Mammoth Cave, Kentucky: The Mammoth Cave National Park Association, p 21.

191 Morrison, George D., *New Entrance to Mammoth Cave*, pp 7–13.

192 United States Circuit Court of Appeals, Sixth Circuit. Transcript of Record. Wyatt and Janin *vs.* Mammoth Cave Development Company. 1927, pp 8, 10.

193 *What the Mammoth Cave Guides Have to Say About the Pretended "New Entrance" Four Miles East From Green River*, STATEMENT OF THE GUIDES. Mammoth Cave National Park manuscript collection.

194 United States Circuit Court of Appeals, Sixth Circuit. Transcript of Record. Wyatt and Janin vs. Mammoth Cave Development Company. 1927, p 44.

195 *Ibid,* p 28.

196 *Ibid.*

197 Goode, Cecil E., 1986. *World Wonder Saved, How Mammoth Cave Became a National Park.* Mammoth Cave, Kentucky: The Mammoth Cave National Park Association, p 27.

198 "Trust Agreement From Mary Jesup Sitgreaves, *et al.* To Fidelity

& Columbia Trust Co. Wm. E. Wyatt and Violet Blair Janin, As Trustees, Creating The Mammoth Cave Trust Estate," 1926, pp 3–4.

199 Goode, Cecil E., 1986. *World Wonder Saved, How Mammoth Cave Became a National Park*. Mammoth Cave, Kentucky: The Mammoth Cave National Park Association, pp 32–33.

200 Barren County Courthouse Book 91. January, 1932, pp 228–229.

201 Nimrod, 1931. "Flint Ridge," *Edmonson County News*, February 26, 1931.

202 Person communication with George McCombs, Munfordville, Kentucky, February, 1999.

203 Goode, Cecil E., 1986. *World Wonder Saved, How Mammoth Cave Became a National Park*. Mammoth Cave, Kentucky: The Mammoth Cave National Park Association.

204 Brucker, Roger W. and Richard A. Watson, 1980. *The Longest Cave*. New York: Alfred A. Knopf, pp 208–209, 2 42–246.

205 "What is the World Heritage Convention?" 1982. Eastern National Park and Monument Association.

Index